THE
SPOTLIGHT
OF
FAITH

THE SPOTLIGHT OF FAITH

WHAT IT MEANS TO WALK WITH GOD

BILL CROWDER

DISCOVERY HOUSE
PUBLISHERS®

Discovery House Publishers is affiliated with RBC Ministries, Grand Rapids, Michigan.

Requests for permission to quote from this book should be directed to: Permissions Department, Discovery House Publishers, P.O. Box 3566, Grand Rapids, MI 49501 or contact us by e-mail at permissionsdept@dhp.org.

Book design and composition by Lakeside Design Plus

Library of Congress Cataloging-in-Publication Data

Crowder, Bill.
    The spotlight of faith : what it means to walk with God / Bill Crowder.
        p. cm.
    ISBN 1-57293-127-2
    1. Christian life—Biblical teaching. 2. Bible—Criticism, interpretation, etc. I. Title.
    BS680.C47C77 2004
    220.9'2—dc22

                                                                2004022933
Printed in the United States of America
Ninth printing 2012

To my wife, Marlene,
who has always been worthy of the spotlight,
but content to stay offstage.
Thank you for living the drama of life with me.

CONTENTS

7

Acknowledgments

In a world full of writers, I find myself in the challenging position of being a speaker. After spending over twenty years in pastoral ministry, the Lord opened a wonderful door of service at RBC Ministries that has stretched and challenged me in ways I never could have imagined apart from that opportunity. Because of that stretching, it is very important to say a word of thanks to people who are trying to teach me the art of words on a page. I cannot express strongly enough my gratitude for their patience during this fascinating process.

Thanks go first of all to Carol Holquist, publisher of Discovery House Publishers, for taking a chance on me and my material. I appreciate your kindness. Also, my gratitude to Judith Markham, the queen of editorial, for her patient help in shaping and reshaping, thinking and rethinking, the chapters of this book. I can't imagine a better supporter and encourager through this project. I also appreciate Bob DeVries, senior publisher of DHP, who first gave me encouragement to learn how to write. Thanks, Bob. To Kathie Schiedel, Melissa Wade, and Judy Grothause, thanks for all you do to help keep the wheels of Discovery House turning. I also want to thank Mart De Haan and Dave Sper of RBC Ministries for the opportunity to start learning the craft of writing through the Discovery Series booklets that RBC produces. It is a privilege to be part of such a great organization.

Additionally, I want to express my gratitude for the work of men like Herbert Lockyer and A. T. Robertson, whose books on character studies have been foundational in helping me to recognize the value of studying a person's life as it is unfolded in the Scriptures. Lockyer's "All" series, particularly *All the Men of the Bible* and *All the Women of the Bible,* are priceless parts of my library, as is Robertson's *Minor Characters in the New Testament.* I have learned much from these godly men, and am thankful for their abiding influence.

Beyond those folks, I want to express my appreciation to my wife, Marlene, who has endured my preaching for almost thirty years and has been a partner in ministry through three churches and now in my new responsibilities at RBC. Beautiful inside and out, Marlene is the best. Thanks, hon. Thanks also to our children (Matt, Beth, Steve, Andy, and Mark) for giving me space when I needed it to get the next chapter done. Finally, to my parents, Earl and Bee Crowder, who never gave up on a wayward son. Mom, though Dad is in heaven, his influence and yours continue to help shape my life and to point the way.

Introduction

Andy Warhol, pop artist and cultural icon back in the 1960s and 70s, said that "in the future everyone will be world-famous for fifteen minutes." If that is true, then in August of 2000, Bob May got his fifteen minutes. In the 2000 PGA Championship, Bob, a largely unknown journeyman golfer, took center stage alongside Tiger Woods, the greatest golfer on the planet. In one of the most dramatic tournaments in years, Bob stood in one of the game's brightest spotlights and played Tiger shot for shot, putt for putt, and hole for hole. At the end of the regulation seventy-two holes of play, they were still deadlocked.

The battle lasted late into the evening as they had to play an additional three holes before the match was won, and the greatest golfer in the world had finally defeated a man who was "nobody from nowhere." Following that tournament, Bob May drifted back into golfing obscurity, but for his "fifteen minutes" he was one of the best in the world.

Similarly, in 2003, another relative unknown, Hilary Lunke, battled the best and best-known women golfers in the world at Pumpkin Ridge, Oregon, to finally win the prestigious U. S. Women's Open in a Monday playoff that was filled with drama, tension, and clutch putting. To this day, Lunke's only win on the LPGA tour is the most significant tournament in women's golf. In fact, prior to her win at the Open, she had never even contended for a tournament title—and has not contended since. Though a steady, solid player, Hilary has not again risen to the level of greatness she enjoyed that sun-splashed day at Pumpkin Ridge. As one wire story put it, "Her only goal when she joined the tour in 2002 was to win one tournament, to have one week that would always be special no matter what happened the rest of her career." It was her moment in the spotlight.

Others may be fascinated and even infatuated with Tiger Woods and Annika Sorenstam, but I'm intrigued by Bob May and Hilary Lunke, with their brief moment in the sun, because there are many more of them in this world than there are superstars. The Bob Mays and Hilary Lunkes of this world are less publicized, but they have fascinating stories of their own to tell, if for a moment we would divert our gaze from the supernova stars who spend their lives on the front pages of the papers, or as the lead items on *SportsCenter*.

In our study of the Bible, we often do the same thing. We focus on the Peters, Pauls, Daniels, and Davids, but lose sight of the fact that the Bible is a book that records the stories of many, many other people. Though they appear on the biblical stage for only a moment or an event or an episode, there is an enormous amount that we can learn from their lives. We can learn lessons about relationships, character, defeat, and failure. We can gain insight on obedience, rebellion, sacrifice, and selfishness.

This book proposes to bring some of those lesser lights to the center of the stage, shine the spotlight on them, and see what we can learn from their experiences. Some were men and some were women. Some lived in the Old Testament era and others in the days of the New Testament. Some were pillars of faith, while others were disobedient. But in each instance, these are the stories of real people, flawed and imperfect, sometimes failing and sometimes succeeding greatly . . . like us, perhaps? As "regular" people who spend more of our lives in the shadows than we do in the spotlight, these are our kind of folks.

It is perfectly appropriate to admire the skill and athleticism of the Tiger Woodses of the world, but most of us really are a lot more like Bob May and Hilary Lunke. So in the following pages let's explore some of these lives and see the profound lessons that are tucked away there for us. All we need to do is redirect the stage lighting and look at the persons who are off to the side or in the wings, instead of in the middle of the stage.

1
Andrew

THE OTHER BROTHER

Bobby (Robert F.) Kennedy was one of the more remarkable people of the twentieth century. Born into a family of power, privilege, wealth, and influence, he graduated from Harvard, completed law school, and became the silent, serious force behind his brother John's political rise. Serving as John F. Kennedy's close confidant, Bobby supported him in his role as senator, masterminded his presidential campaign, and then (reluctantly) served under him as Attorney General of the United States, leading an aggressive fight against organized crime and against racial bigotry in America. After his brother's assassination in 1963, Bobby left his position as attorney general and began looking for his own place to make a difference in the world. He became active in the civil rights movement of the 1960s, worked tirelessly against poverty in America, and in 1966 was elected senator from the state of New York. Then, in 1968, when he was the leading candidate for the Democratic presidential nomination, Bobby, like his brother before him, was assassinated. He was only forty-two years old.

By any normal standard, Bobby Kennedy lived a remarkable life. Yet the standards he faced were anything but normal. Why? Because he wasn't Joe and he wasn't John. His oldest brother, Joe, Jr., was a war hero who, before being killed in combat in World War II, had been handpicked by their powerful father, Joseph Sr., to be the "Kennedy president." His older brother John was also a war hero, and he actually did become the president. Bobby was the third son, and although he was a talented, accomplished, and powerful man in his own right, he never seemed to be good enough. He could never be the giant that he had helped John to become—a fact that biographers say was a sore point between Bobby and his father. At the same time, it seems that Bobby Kennedy also carried the weight of his own expectations, feeling that he could never quite measure up to the lofty standards established by his older, taller, more handsome, more heroic, more charismatic brothers. His relatively short life was lived in their long and substantial shadows.

Anyone who has older brothers or sisters can probably relate to Bobby Kennedy's experience. Being the younger brother or sister gives true meaning to the term "sibling rivalry," especially when you hear comments like, "Why can't you be like Jim?" or "Aren't you Amy's kid sister?" or "Your brother Sam is an honor student—what happened to you?" or "Did Sarah get all the good looks in your family?" As one cynic has said, "The dream that all men should live as brothers is held by men who have no brothers."

It can be difficult, and more than a little exasperating, to follow in another's footsteps, or to be continually compared to someone else. Perhaps it was this kind of experience that prompted the rock band, the Guess Who, to sing about "no hand-me-down shoes . . . no hand-me-down clothes . . . no hand-me-down love." Being a younger sibling can be tough.

No one knew this better than Andrew, Simon Peter's younger brother. So let's allow him to step out of the shadows and onto center stage where we can see him more clearly.

"Behold the Lamb!"

Andrew is first seen as a disciple of the desert prophet John the Baptist, who was preaching a message of repentance and kingdom hope unlike anything ever heard by the people of Israel who were living under the occupying forces of the powerful Roman Empire. Mark's gospel pictures John as a throwback, more reminiscent of the Old Testament than the New. He fascinated people with his simple lifestyle and his dramatic proclamations against sin. When he spoke, people were electrified. They listened and then responded with obedience and a submission to baptism, symbolizing their repentance. Crowds followed John everywhere. His charismatic ministry brought hope to the common people and became a threat to the leaders of the nation—a threat that would ultimately cost John his life. Among the followers who hung on his every word was Andrew, a young man from Capernaum, and his friend John.

When John the Baptist stood in the muddy water at the southern end of the Jordan River, baptizing his followers and preaching to them about the coming Messiah, the line of people waiting for baptism extended as far as the eye could see. One by one, people responded to John's powerful message by accepting baptism, which acknowledged their need of spiritual rescue and symbolized the forgiveness of their sins. Though this baptism carried no inherent saving power, it was viewed as an act of spiritual cleansing for the repentant.

As the line of people snaked its way forward into the water, John's mood suddenly changed. He had spied a familiar face in the waiting crowd. "Behold," he called, "the Lamb of God who takes away the sin of the world!" (John 1:29). After introducing his followers to Jesus of Nazareth, John pronounced these compelling words: "This is the One who baptizes in the Holy Spirit. I myself have seen, and have testified that this is the Son of God" (vv. 33–34).

The young man from Capernaum must have been stunned. He had seen the power of John the Baptist's ministry up close and personal; he had watched the multitudes respond to his message. But now, when John baptized Jesus, Andrew and the others saw and heard something even more astonishing: "Behold, the heavens were opened, and he saw the Spirit of God descending as a dove and lighting on Him, and behold, a voice out of the heavens, said 'This is My beloved Son, in whom I am well-pleased'" (Matthew 3:16–17). Something unusual was happening in the waters of the Jordan that day!

Andrew had just been introduced to the Son of God. The Messiah long foretold. The One who would offer mankind a relationship with God based on divine love and forgiveness instead of religious ceremony and ritual. The One who had come to become the Lamb of sacrifice.

Andrew did not hesitate. He immediately believed John's declaration that Jesus was God's offer of salvation and began to follow Him (John 1:37–40), thus becoming part of the apostolic band. In fact, Andrew and his friend were the first two disciples Jesus called (although Andrew's friend is not named, scholars have always believed that he was the author of John's gospel).

The depth of Andrew's belief and commitment would be expressed in his very first act as a follower of Jesus, and confirmed in the ongoing pattern of his life!

Andrew's Passion for People

As a pastor, I often said, "I never cease to be amazed at the things people choose to be passionate about." From the color of the Sunday church bulletin to the color of the carpet. From the temperature in the sanctuary to the choice of flowers for the front of the church. From the importance of choir robes to a staunch conviction that choir robes are unscriptural. I once had a lengthy conversation with an irate church member over the communion bread. The cause of his distress was that we had switched the communion bread from broken crackers to unleavened bread. No matter how many different ways I tried to explain that, while there was nothing wrong with using the broken crackers and we simply wanted the congregation to experience the Lord's Table in a manner similar to the experience of the early church, this person would not be calmed or convinced. He wanted his crackers back! It never ceases to amaze me what people choose to be passionate about.

You can learn a lot about people by identifying what it is they are passionate about, and Andrew is no exception. He was passionate about the eternal destiny of human beings. This was not just a concern for people in general; it

19

was concern for individual persons and where they would spend eternity. Andrew expressed this passion immediately after he began following the Savior when the first thing he did was to find his own brother and tell him about Jesus.

HIS BROTHER

Most of us who know Christ often feel inadequate and more than a bit nervous when it comes to sharing our faith. Yet Andrew's first act of discipleship was to share his faith. And the difficulty of that declaration was intensified by the object of his outreach, because Andrew was trying to share Christ with:

- The one closest to him, his older brother.
- The one who may have been most unreachable (remember Peter's legendary temper!).
- The one whose shadow he had lived in his entire life!

Our family members can be the hardest people to reach with the message of the gospel. Why? Because they know us so well. They have heard or borne the brunt of our unkind or inappropriate words and they have seen our selfish acts. They often know about our secret desires and have witnessed our private anger.

When I became a Christian in 1973, it was after a number of years in which my personal faith could best be described as "churchianity." I claimed to be a person of faith, went to church, was active in church activities, sang in the choir, and was quite proud of my religiosity. In fact, I was so good at religion that almost everyone who knew me was convinced that I was "a good Christian." Well, almost everyone.

My brother Rob, who is two years my junior, saw through my act and recognized my hypocrisy. So when I did come to Christ, it was virtually impossible for me to share my faith with Rob because he had seen the reality of my life in contrast to my previous religious claims. At one point, the friction between us became so intense that when I would enter a room, Rob would leave. It was a long time before my brother could accept my claims of being a follower of Christ—and then it was only after he saw enough genuine change in my life as evidence of it. Now, years later, Rob also is a believer and we have a wonderful relationship. But those early days of my faith journey created a tension between us because he knew me so well.

As a man with a newfound faith, Andrew could have chosen a much easier target for his first proclamation of the gospel. Yet he began with the most difficult: the person closest to him, his brother Simon. Andrew wanted so much for his brother to know Jesus that he went to him with the message that every Jew had longed to proclaim for centuries, "We have found the Messiah" (John 1:41).

The results of Andrew's proclamation were twofold:

- A great apostle was born. (Remember, you never know what will become of one life and the difference that life can make.)
- A great example was begun. (Here we see the first true New Testament example of *evangelism*: someone bringing someone else to Jesus Christ.)

When Andrew reached out to Simon, he had no idea what the future held for his big brother. He did not know that Simon would become Peter, and that Peter would become the apostle who would be Christ's principal instrument in giving birth to the church. Nor did Andrew have any idea that his brother, an uneducated fisherman, would someday write two books that would be part of the scriptures that became the New Testament. Andrew simply wanted his brother to know Christ.

Remember: the toughest to reach (our own family) still need to be reached! But Andrew did not confine his evangelism to those closest to him.

A CHILD

Anyone we bring to the Savior could become like Simon Peter—a true spiritual diamond in the rough. Each new believer has the potential to become a powerful instrument in the hands of a powerful God. This is probably most evident in those who come to faith in Christ in their youth and immaturity. As someone once said, an older person who comes to the Savior has only a soul to give to Christ; a child who comes to faith has not only a soul but a life to give to the Lord.

This is why I have always had such great appreciation for people who are passionate about children's ministry or youth work. I love my own kids, but I must confess that other people's kids can easily drive me a little nutty (actually even my own can do this at times). I have no doubt that my personality and gifts are geared toward adult ministry. Yet adult ministry is no more significant than ministry to children and teens. In fact, few things are quite as exciting as youth ministry, because we cannot predict what form these unshaped lives will grow into or how God might work in them and through them. The possibilities seem almost as infinite as God Himself. And it would seem that, at some level, Andrew may have recognized this, as evidenced by the event recorded in John 6:1–14.

At this point in Jesus' ministry, a huge crowd, perhaps as many as 25,000 people, had been following Him to hear Him preach and watch His miracles. They were so captivated by Him that they even forgot to pack their picnic lunches, and after several hours these folks were getting hungry. Unfortunately, there were no Burger Kings or fast-food falafels on the Galilean hillsides. So for Jesus' fledgling disciples, this offered a wonderful "teachable moment."

Jesus tested Philip by asking him where they could buy enough bread to feed such a crowd (John 6:5). Philip's response seemed to be half-despair and half-sarcasm: "If we spent 200 denarii [a year's wages for a day-laborer], it wouldn't be enough to give each of them even a taste!"

Then Andrew entered the scene. And I find it interesting that, even at the moment that Andrew steps to center stage to "save the day," the writer feels compelled to remind us that Andrew was "Simon Peter's brother." Even in the spotlight Andrew was still in his big brother's shadow (John 6:8).

Andrew had a hungry multitude and an ill-prepared group of disciples, and what he did must have seemed laughable to anyone who understood the scale of the problem. He brought a boy and his sack lunch to Jesus (John 6:9). "There is a lad here who has five barley loaves and two fish," he said. Yet even to Andrew this seemed woefully inadequate: "But what are these for so many people?"

Now came the teachable moment, and it was a lesson the Twelve needed to learn. As the hymnwriter put it, "Little is much when God is in it." Jesus took the meager lunch of bread and fish and multiplied it to feed the entire crowd! He not only fed them; He gave them all they could eat (John 6:11). He not only gave them all they could eat; He provided so bountifully that they had twelve baskets of leftovers (John 6:12). Upon seeing this miracle, the people could not help but acknowledge, "This is truly the Prophet who is to come into the world" (John 6:14).

All of this happened because Andrew brought one small, seemingly insignificant boy to Jesus. How many others had overlooked this boy, even ignored him? But Andrew took him to Jesus. Amazing.

Once again, Andrew's solution to the problem was very simple: bring someone to Jesus.

- He went after someone insignificant.
- He engaged a child to help.
- He watched Jesus take something small and bless it, multiply it, and use it.

Even as a young follower in the faith, Andrew seems to have learned something that all of us need to remember. We reach people not because of what they can do for Jesus, but for what He can do in and through them! This means:

- We must reach the insignificant as well as the mighty.
- We must be committed to reaching children.

- We must see the multitudes through the eyes of Jesus and allow Him to take our weak efforts and bless, multiply, and use them to reach people.

A GROUP OF GENTILES

By now, among the disciples, Andrew seems to have been regarded as the one who understood bringing people to Jesus. We see this clearly when Jesus and His men were in Jerusalem for the feast of Passover.

Passover was one of the three "high feast" times of the year for the Jewish people (along with the Feast of Weeks and the Day of Atonement), and they made pilgrimages from all over the world to come to the temple in Jerusalem to celebrate those feasts. As a result, the city was filled with people who had come to worship. Many Gentiles also had heard of this new rabbi and wanted to see and hear Him for themselves, but Gentiles were barred from entering the teaching place of the temple. When Gentiles visited the temple, they were allowed only in the outer court; the inner temple court was reserved for Jewish men. As a result, the Gentiles were cut off from the teaching of Jesus, the healer from Nazareth (John 12:20–22).

The Gentiles asked Philip for an audience with Jesus, and Philip then turned to Andrew to get the job done. Perhaps Philip felt uncomfortable or even uncertain about the appropriateness of bringing hated Gentiles to the Christ. What he was certain about, however, was that Andrew would know what to do. So Philip took the Gentiles' appeal to Andrew, who did not hesitate to take their request to the Lord.

This adds a new wrinkle to Andrew's ministry, for here we see that Andrew has moved beyond his own family, and even beyond his own people to reach across racial and cultural barriers. Andrew responded with compassion and concern for those outside his comfort zone, outside the scope of the conventional thinking of his day, outside what was considered "proper." Andrew was not afraid to take a risk if necessary to bring people to Christ.

This is the heart of missions: taking Christ to every tribe, tongue, nation, and people. As messengers of the gospel we are called to reach out to every ethnic group, to stretch across every cultural barrier. We don't minister just to the people who look and talk and think like us. This is not a terribly complicated concept, but it is an eternally important one—and it was Andrew who blazed the trail for us. It was Andrew who modeled a passion and compassion for other people to know and find what he had embraced in Jesus.

Andrew's Opportunity to Grow

Baseball is a great game, filled with strategy, drama, and action. Baseball is also considered "the great American pastime." One of the things that makes baseball so "all-American"—at least in my opinion—is the number of brothers who usually are playing in the major leagues at the same time. When I was growing up, the Boyer brothers (Ken and Clete) were part of the game. Both were excellent players with outstanding careers, but Ken played for the Cardinals—in the pinstriped shadow of his brother's vaunted New York Yankees dynasty.

I imagine them as kids playing catch in the backyard, pretending to be playing together in the seventh and deciding game of the World Series. I also imagine that these guys ratcheted up the intensity and competition level as brother tried to surpass and outdo brother. Who would hit the most home runs? Who would hit the longest home runs? Who would be drafted first, sign a contract, make it to the major leagues, win a playoff? Sibling rivalry at its best and worst. Best, because there is nothing quite like the friendly but intense competition between brothers. Worst, because inevitably one brother will surpass the other in ability, success, and acclaim.

Recognizing the volatility of sibling rivalry, we must also recognize the great potential for friction between Andrew and Simon Peter, even though both were disciples of the Master. Andrew was the first to come to Jesus, and he lost no time in bringing his brother Peter to Jesus; yet he was excluded from the inner circle of the Master's disciples (Peter, James, and John). This inner circle witnessed the raising of Jairus's daughter from the dead, the Transfiguration of Jesus, and the agony and horror of the Gethsemane experience. The inner circle saw it all.

James and John also were brothers, but both of them were included in the circle. Peter and Andrew were brothers, yet Andrew was excluded.

Only once in the gospel records do we find Andrew included with this intimate group of three, and that was a time when they began to question Jesus regarding His teaching. The result was what would become known as the Olivet Discourse, second only to the Sermon on the Mount in its length and significance among the sermons of the Lord. In being included at that one special moment of opportunity, Andrew was allowed to hear some of the most significant things the Savior taught.

- He heard about Christ's return.
- He heard about the coming judgment, its consequences, and the need for the world to hear the message of Christ.
- He heard about the trials and triumph in the sufferings of God's people and the victorious return of the Savior.
- He heard about the integrity and trustworthiness of the Word of God.

Andrew was allowed to see the curtain drawn back and privileged to hear teachings that remain critical to our own faith experience today. Knowing the hope of Christ's return promises us a better day ahead, while the reminder of the consequences of sin and judgment urge and motivate us to share with others the message of Christ's forgiveness. The truth of the enduring Word of God gives us foundation for all of our thinking and living.

Andrew got to hear these powerful truths from the lips of the Savior Himself! He had been faithful in sharing the message of Christ, the message of hope, to everyone who crossed his path. Now, the Master honored that faithfulness by telling him something powerful: what he, Andrew, was doing and modeling in his evangelistic efforts would ultimately be multiplied into a global mission, all for the purpose of doing what Andrew did—bringing people to Christ before it is too late!

Peter and John shared the truths Jesus taught them by writing letters that would become part of the New Testament. "As for Andrew," writes Herbert Lockyer, "we can be confident that, as one whose ministry was personal and not public, his lips were not silent as to what he heard and learned during that wonderful teaching session" (Herbert Lockyer, *All the Apostles of the Bible* [Grand Rapids, Mich.: Zondervan Publishing House, 1972], 53).

◆

After the Olivet Discourse, Andrew appears only one other time in the pages of Scripture, and that is in the list of the disciples present in the upper room, awaiting the coming of the Holy Spirit at Pentecost (Acts 1). Then, after these brief moments in the sun, he quietly returned to the shadows as his big brother, Peter, stepped back onto center stage. According to early church tradition, Andrew gave his life for the message of the cross; it was his passion. After spending his days preaching in Jerusalem, Andrew reportedly was hung on an X-shaped cross, known ever since as St. Andrew's Cross (Herbert Lockyer, *All the Men of the Bible* [Grand Rapids, Mich.: Zondervan Publishing House, 1958], 49).

Andrew is, undoubtedly, an overlooked individual in the message and ministry of the church. But he was not, and will not be, overlooked by the Master he loved, served, and proclaimed. No, Andrew was not the Billy Graham of his day. That role went to his brother Peter. Instead, Andrew was more like Edward Kimball.

Edward Kimball, a young Sunday school teacher in Boston, had a burden for boys to come to the Savior. One day he shared Christ with a young shoe salesman named D. L. Moody, who was used by God to touch two nations, England and America, with the gospel as he preached in powerful evangelistic campaigns and founded the Moody Bible Institute in Chicago. Under Moody's ministry, Wilbur Chapman, who became a great evangelist in his own generation, turned to the Savior, and God used Chapman's preaching to

29

reach a wild young Chicago White Stockings baseball player named Billy Sunday. Sunday became a believer and gave his life to serving Christ as an evangelist. Under Sunday's ministry, a young man named Mordecai Hamm came to Christ, and Hamm's ministry of evangelism was greatly used by God in the southeastern part of the United States. In one of Hamm's evangelistic meetings a youth named Billy Graham met the Savior. All because of Edward Kimball, an Andrew who shared his faith with one young man who crossed his path. (Adapted from Joseph Stowell, *Following Christ* [Chicago: Moody Press, 1996], 130–131.)

For every Simon Peter, apostle Paul, Martin Luther, and Billy Graham, we are grateful. But we should never underestimate the impact of the Andrews—or the Edward Kimballs—who work quietly behind the scenes to reach one heart at a time. They may never be in the spotlight, but great will be their reward in heaven.

PRINCIPLES FROM THE LIFE OF ANDREW

◆ Sharing your faith begins with a desire for other people to find what you have found in Christ.

◆ Sharing your faith displays concern for those closest to you, as well as for those who are viewed as insignificant by the world.

◆ Sharing your faith requires that you be willing to call anyone and everyone to the knowledge of the Savior.

◆ Sharing your faith requires an understanding that Jesus came to die for the world, and you, like Andrew, must live to reach the world.

2
Barnabas

THE ENCOURAGER

Nicknames. When you're a kid, they can make you cringe in embarrassment and mortification or puff you up with pride and self-satisfaction. Lefty, Shorty, Stretch, Brainiac—there's no end to the monikers kids can place on each other, either flattering or demeaning.

Having worn glasses since the fifth grade, I long ago grew accustomed to being called "four-eyes," but that's not the worst name I've been called. In the summer between the seventh and eighth grades, I was pole-vaulting with a chopped-down sapling when my pole broke. So did my right wrist. Being condemned to spend the summer months with a cast on my arm was bad enough, but when school began that August, things got exponentially worse as the story of my misadventure quickly spread through the halls of St. Albans Junior High School. I became an instant target. First came the relentless ribbing, which was bad enough. But then a friend (at least I think he was a friend) who knew my middle name (Earl) dubbed me with a nickname that would stick with me for years. It was . . . are you ready for this? . . . "Earl Squirrel the Pole-Vaulter." Now, aside from the lyric poetry that this produced, I have no earthly idea how the squirrel part got in there. But I was Earl Squirrel well into my high school career. Nicknames.

The practice of conferring nicknames is not at all new. Nor is it the sole property of the young. In fact, the apostles of Jesus Christ gave a special nickname to a member of the early church in Jerusalem that we would do well to aspire to. His real name was Joseph, but his nickname was "Barnabas," which means "the son of encouragement."

At a Bible conference some years ago, I heard Scott Dixon of Cedarville College say that this name meant that Joseph/Barnabas was committed to being a carpenter in a world of termites! I think that is a terrific analogy, and one that we see lived out as we watch Joseph/Barnabas step into the spotlight on the center stage of the biblical story.

We first meet him in Acts 4: "Now Joseph, a Levite of Cyprian birth, who was also called Barnabas by the apostles (which translated means Son of Encouragement), and who owned a tract of land, sold it and brought the money and laid it at the apostles' feet" (vv. 36–37).

It seems certain that the disciples nicknamed Joseph "the Son of Encouragement" because of his temperament, his attitude toward others, and his ministry as a believer. Encouragement was so much the overriding characteristic of his life that it was just natural to call him that. Unlike Four-Eyes or Earl Squirrel the Pole-Vaulter, Joseph's nickname reflected the passion of his heart.

As we are introduced to Barnabas, we also learn several other interesting things about this man.

- He was close to the apostles. In the midst of a large and growing early church, he was known and appreciated by the leadership. They acknowledged and promoted his ministry.
- He was a Levite. "A Levite of Cyprian birth" tells us that Barnabas was Jewish, and, specifically, of the priestly tribe of Israel. Whether he was trained in the priestly ministry we do not know, but Luke's record recognizes his priestly lineage.
- He was a Cyprian. Though apparently now living in Palestine, his birthplace was the island of Cyprus in the Mediterranean.
- He was generous. Barnabas gave all he had to the work of the church, not only giving himself in service to others, but also giving financially. His generosity, as his life showed, was the true expression of his heart, similar to the church at Corinth, which Paul described this way: "For I bear witness that according to their ability, yes, and beyond their ability, they were freely willing, imploring us with much urgency that we would receive the gift and the fellowship of the ministering to the saints. And this they did, as we had hoped, but first gave themselves to the Lord, and then to us by the will of God" (2 Corinthians 8:3–5 NKJV).

These believers gave themselves first, and then gave of what they had. This seems to perfectly describe Barnabas.

For him, giving was the pattern of his life, not the exception to the rule. Thus, Barnabas, who gave himself away in service and care to others, is a powerful reminder of the value of being a carpenter in a world of spiritual and emotional termites. Three times he stepped forward and acted, and all three times he lived up to his name.

Encouraging a Young Believer

Wendell and Pat had been visiting our new church plant for a few weeks. Admittedly, it took a little bit of effort because the facilities of our young church were not in any way traditional in an area where church was a very traditional thing. To visit a new church can be a daunting thing in the best of circumstances, but to explore an unfamiliar church as a non-Christian can be extremely uncomfortable. When that church defies all the mental images you have of a church it gets even harder—and that was part of what made the challenge so tough for Pat and Wendell. In a community where churches had beautiful brick facades or colonial pillars, our little congregation met in the sewer plant!

When we started the new church, the only available meeting place was the community center in the basement of the local water and sewer plant, and that created a stigma for some people when invited to join us for worship. Our folks worked hard at bringing visitors, but often got pretty skeptical looks when they told their friends or family members where we met. Yet Pat and Wendell came, week after week, without any apparent qualms about our unconventional church home.

Then, on Easter Sunday 1980, Wendell and Pat gave their hearts and their home to Christ. As a new Christian, Wendell was a spiritual sponge. He couldn't get enough of the Word or of spiritual service. He and I would go on visitation together, would engage in work projects together, and would study the Scriptures and pray together. Watching Wendell grow has been one of the singular joys of my ministry. After several years of spiritual growth, he became one of our deacons and remained a member of the leadership team long after the Lord had moved my family to another ministry in a distant state. The interesting thing was that the more I encouraged Wendell, the more encouraged I was about the work of the ministry in his heart. His spiritual desires fed my own heart. Though separated by many miles, our friendship has endured for over twenty years, and I never see Wendell and Pat without marveling at what God has done in their lives.

In some small way, this experience in my own life helps me relate to Barnabas. He was also concerned about encouraging and building up a young believer. He took it even further, however, by being willing to take a risk in ministry when he took under his wing a man the rest of the community of faith viewed with skepticism.

Young Saul of Tarsus had a history of persecuting believers, so it's not surprising that he was greatly feared by the believers in the church of Jerusalem. Saul stood by approvingly as Stephen was stoned to death (Acts 7:54–8:1). He had traveled throughout Palestine hounding the followers of Christ and causing them great suffering. "As for Saul," recorded Luke, "he made havoc of the church, entering every house, and dragging off men and women, committing them to prison" (Acts 8:3 NKJV). Not a pretty picture.

Then, a great transformation took place when Saul had his "Damascus road experience" and knelt in faith before the very Savior whose followers he had been persecuting. The young firebrand was on his way to the city of Damascus to root out even more of these "dangerous" Christians when a bright light appeared, knocking him to the ground. In Acts 9:4 we read that a voice spoke to him saying, "Saul, Saul, why are you persecuting Me?" Saul had enough sense to recognize this as some kind of a divine encounter, and responded, "Who are You, Lord?" (NKJV). The answer must have shaken him to his core: "I am Jesus, whom you are persecuting" (Acts 9:5). To Saul's shock, the group he was trying to drive out of existence was right, after all! He immediately abandoned his mission of persecution and began a new life—a life of following the Christ he had resisted so long and so hard.

Great, right? Not to the church in Jerusalem. They simply couldn't believe that this man had truly come to the Savior. Like the claims to faith of Charles Colson, the famed and feared "hatchet man" of the Nixon White House of the 1970s, it seemed too improbable to believe. Saul come to Christ? Not possible. Not even for the grace of God. As a result, when Saul arrived in Jerusalem, "he tried to join the disciples; but they were all afraid of him, and did not believe that he was a disciple" (Acts 9:26 NKJV).

I can certainly understand the fear and skepticism of the Jerusalem church after the pain and suffering Saul had inflicted. Why wouldn't they suspect that this was just an attempt to infiltrate the church in order to create more mayhem? Yet Barnabas believed that Saul's conversion was genuine, and he acted on that belief. "Barnabas took him and brought him to the apostles. And he declared to them how he had seen the Lord on the road, and that He had spoken to him, and how he had preached boldly at Damascus in the name of Jesus. So he was with them at Jerusalem, coming in and going out" (Acts 9:27–28 NKJV).

Taking a stand like this isn't easy. You know your own heart but you cannot clearly know what is in the heart of another person. Sometimes people disappoint you; sometimes they betray you. Sometimes you get burned badly. All of these results were possibilities when Barnabas reached out to this new convert, living out his convictions about caring for others. Barnabas disregarded any of these possible negative consequences because, I believe, he was convinced that:

- It was better to err on the side of compassion than on the side of judgment.
- It was better to try and fail than not to try.
- It was better to invest in others, even at the risk of losing that investment.

At a time when the church wanted nothing to do with Saul of Tarsus, Barnabas stepped in where angels feared to tread. He invested his time, effort, and encouragement in young Saul, and that investment paid a huge return for the body of Christ. Saul of Tarsus became Paul the Apostle, who:

- Grew in boldness and credibility. As the leadership of the church in Jerusalem validated Paul's ministry, he became accepted and recognized as a potential leader in his own right. At least a portion of this credibility initially came from their recognition of Barnabas's confidence in him.

- Gained a ministry unparalleled in the early church. The early church knew no greater church planter than Paul. His missionary journeys have formed the primer on outreach ministry that the church has followed for some 2,000 years.

- Wrote most of the New Testament. Paul's rabbinical training, as well as his truly brilliant mind, became instruments of God as the Holy Spirit inspired him in the crafting of at least a dozen books in the New Testament, far more than any other writer. His letters to the early churches ranged from matters of deep doctrinal precision (Romans, Ephesians) to practical Christian living (Philippians, Philemon) to church leadership (1 and 2 Timothy, Titus). His writings changed the way the church understood and explained Christian truth.

- Learned how to invest in others, too. Paul learned firsthand how one person's investment can change a life; and what Barnabas did for him, Paul likewise did for others. Men like Timothy, Titus, Onesimus, and Epaphroditus and women like Phoebe, Priscilla, and Lydia became leaders in the community of faith because Paul invested in them.

All of this was an ongoing extension of Barnabas's investment in Paul! A powerful return on his investment—wouldn't you agree?

The lesson of Barnabas is clear. You can either waste time on secondary things, or invest time in others!

Encouraging a Young Church

Barnabas was concerned about building up young believers in the faith and encouraging potential church leaders, but he didn't stop there. He also had a burden for the spiritual development of a young church at large.

Luke does not nail down the date, but it was probably in the late thirties or early forties of the first century when the church at Jerusalem heard about a powerful revival in the city of Antioch (Acts 11:19–26). Antioch was a Syrian community on the Mediterranean coast about two hundred miles north of Israel, near the southern edge of Asia Minor (modern-day Turkey). The church leadership responded by sending a representative to Antioch to both investigate the events and to respond appropriately. "The news about them reached the ears of the church at Jerusalem, and they sent Barnabas off to Antioch" (Acts 11:22).

Knowing what we do about Barnabas, it is not surprising that the church leaders in Jerusalem sent him. With his established track record of encouragement, he was the ideal person to care for the congregation at Antioch. There he expanded his ministry of help and encouragement, and provides us with a picture of how these elements of ministry can impact a local church family. This begins with what he saw in Antioch and how he reacted to it.

HIS REACTION

We live in a day when it's not cool to get excited about the things of Christ. Although there is a rising interest in spirituality and the supernatural, people seem increasingly skeptical about organized, institutional Christianity. Even people who claim faith regularly discount its significance or impact on their lives. As one popular musician responded when someone questioned her about her religious beliefs, "Yes, I am a Christian, but don't think that is going to change my act." Somehow, we feel the need to distance ourselves from being perceived as "too religious" or "too Christian."

I remember as a young Christian in Bible college singing with gusto the Bill Gaither song, "Get all excited! Go tell everybody that Jesus Christ is still the King of kings!" My fellow students and I were not embarrassed by our enthusiasm; it seemed the most natural thing in the world to openly celebrate the joy of Christ. Now that I am older, both in years and in faith, I find myself being more measured and perhaps a little more sensitive about how I express my faith. I fear that there have been times when my enthusiasm has come across as arrogant, and that my desires to communicate the gospel have sounded judgmental. Youthful energy misdirected can easily offend the very people we are trying to reach. At the same time, however, I have to say that it wouldn't hurt us to have a little more sanctified enthusiasm once in a while! We can become so careful, so measured, so ambivalent in our living out of the faith that we present a Christianity that offers little to a watching world. A life without enthusiasm and joy is not a life that many people will be drawn to.

Barnabas didn't suffer from a lack of appropriately directed enthusiasm. He was excited by what he saw in Antioch, and he let it show. "When he came and had seen the grace of God, he was glad, and encouraged them all that with purpose of heart they should continue with the Lord" (Acts 11:23 NKJV).

When Barnabas saw the grace of God at work, he rejoiced. Then he immediately got involved in trying to help the new believers in Antioch understand and grow in their faith, encouraging them to faithfully and consistently walk with the Lord. He literally began being "Barnabas" to them!

His Character

We live in a world that is impressed by the spectacular and enamored of the rich, beautiful, famous, and important. In Washington, DC, a person's significance is often measured by the number of people following in his or her wake. Professional boxers are notorious for surrounding themselves with followers who respond to their every beck and call. In the realm of entertainment, some celebrities travel with such a large pack of security personnel, publicists, and, on occasion, hangers-on that it seems they could fill several large buses! Our culture seems to measure significance by the size of the entourage.

Barnabas, however, had no grand entourage, no flashy wardrobe, no dynamic "platform presence." The only platform he had for his ministry was godly character. "For he was a good man, and full of the Holy Spirit and of faith. And considerable numbers were brought to the Lord" (Acts 11:24). Barnabas's heart and life were:

- Full of goodness. Goodness, which is one aspect of the fruit of Spirit, has to do with moral excellence. Barnabas had a heart that truly displayed the essence of the character of Christ Himself and made it visible to the watching world.

41

- Full of the Spirit. Barnabas was a man under the control of the Holy Spirit. Ephesians 5:17–18 describes the control of the Spirit as "a filling," in much the same way that the wind drives a boat by filling its sail. Barnabas's life was filled by, driven by, the Spirit of God.
- Full of faith. Barnabas was committed to trusting God, which also meant being faithful to God. Bible scholars believe that the phrase "full of faith" could refer to either trust or faithfulness, and that in itself is powerful. If it refers to trust, it speaks of a dependence upon God that readily submits to His power rather than seeking to engineer or manipulate results. If it refers to faithfulness, it speaks of a depth of commitment that causes personal abandonment to God—another vivid example of deep faith and trust. In either case, what drove Barnabas was a heart filled with such confidence in God that he was able to live dependently upon the God of His confidence.
- Full of fruit. At the end of the day, Barnabas was not just some otherworldly character who was of little practical value. Ministry that reflects the heart of God is going to be ministry that embraces His priorities and concerns—especially as those concerns relate to people in need of eternal hope. To that end, Barnabas was at work in a hands-on way, being an instrument used by God to bring many people to the Savior through His ministry.

Make no mistake about it. His usefulness was not an accident or happenstance or the result of his being a go-getter or a self-motivated, hard-working overachiever. Barnabas was useful in God's hands *because* he was full of goodness, faith, and the Holy Spirit. His ministry was the product of the character built into his life as a result of faithfully walking with the Savior over the long haul of his life. The spirit of God pouring into Barnabas's life gave him something to pour out to others—and pour out he did!

His Ministry

Barnabas was not a Lone Ranger. (I really appreciate this about him.) He recognized the scope of the work that needed to be done and that he needed others to share the work with him. To that end, he traveled to Tarsus and brought Paul (Saul) in to help. Not only did this advance the work at Antioch, it also gave Paul, still a young believer, an opportunity to gain more training and preparation for his own future ministry.

Additionally, Barnabas was willing to do what it took to see the work in Antioch developed. He invested a year of his life in Antioch, encouraging the Christians there and teaching them the Word, which is still the instrument that God uses to change lives.

Was it worth the effort? Yes! Luke tells us that it was at Antioch that the followers of the Savior were first called "Christians"—literally, "little Christs"! And the believers at Antioch would become one of the strongest congregations of the early church era. This was a direct result of God's ministry through Barnabas there—an investment that paid huge dividends for the glory of God.

Encouraging a Young Failure

All of us fail at one time or another. But it is how we respond to failure that shapes and directs our future lives.

If we allow a moment of failure to define us, we probably will never move beyond it or rise above it. If, however, we embrace such a failure as an opportunity to build Christ into us, the incident can become a stepping-stone to greater usefulness. Many can testify that character and personal strength are not developed in times of ease, but in times of difficulty. We usually learn much more from the failures of life than we do through the successes we enjoy. If we respond properly to the hardships and failures of life we can grow to be more like Christ—the point James was making in James 1, where he reminds us that the hard experiences of life can be spiritually formative in our relationship with Christ. This truth lies at the heart of Barnabas's passion for encouraging John Mark, a young failure who was perilously close to becoming a throwaway (Acts 15:36–40).

Barnabas had a pastor's heart, which may explain why he and Paul had to part ways. Paul had the heart of an evangelist, the mind of a theologian, and the attitude of an Old Testament prophet, while Barnabas demonstrated patience and personal care. It was inevitable that these two men would disagree eventually—and eventually arrived with John Mark's failure.

By this time, Paul had surpassed Barnabas and become the leader of the missionary band. Even the naming of the ministry team had shifted from "Barnabas and Saul" to "Paul and Barnabas." Paul's public gifts of teaching, preaching, and leading had moved him into the role of primary leader of the group. Now Paul wanted to return to the sites of their first missionary journey to check on the progress of the churches that he, Barnabas, and their missionary band had previously planted on their first trip through Asia Minor. That was when the point of contention arose. "Then . . . Paul said to Barnabas, 'Let us now go back and visit our brethren in every city where we have preached the word of the Lord, and see how they are doing.' Now Barnabas was determined to take with them John called Mark" (Acts 15:36–37 NKJV).

Paul disagreed. On the previous journey to Asia Minor, John Mark had bailed out, leaving the team shorthanded, and Paul had not forgotten. Mark had been a believer who had lived in a home that supported and encouraged the work of the early church (Acts 12:12), the home of his mother Mary, who happened to be the sister of Barnabas (Colossians 4:10). Barnabas had undoubtedly been influential in making certain that John Mark accompanied them on the first trip and, apparently, at some point on the trip—which was difficult at best—Mark had decided to return home. Paul had no time for deserters, but Barnabas wanted to give Mark another opportunity to share and grow in the ministry before them. If Paul had a lesson to learn, it was the lesson of being patient with someone's humanity without being accepting of his sin. Barnabas knew how to do this, but it would be years before Paul would learn. As a result, "they had such a sharp disagreement that they parted company" (Acts 15:39 NIV). Thus came the dissolution of the partnership that had begun perhaps as much as fourteen years earlier when Barnabas had defended Paul to the church at Jerusalem and encouraged him in the faith. How strong was the division?

- Barnabas took Mark and left for Cyprus, his own home and birthplace.

- Paul took Silas and headed to Europe, answering the call of the Macedonian vision.

As we saw in the previous section, we know a great deal about the results of Paul's ministry. But what of Barnabas? Well, we never hear of him again in the New Testament, but his commitment to young, inconsistent, undependable John Mark bore fruit that continues to benefit followers of Christ today. His investment in Mark resulted in:

- A strong relationship with Simon Peter. "She who is in Babylon, chosen together with you, sends you her greetings, and so does my son, Mark" (1 Peter 5:13). The apostle Peter referred to Mark as his son, just as Paul did with Timothy!

- A strong ministry that endures. In the gospel of Mark it is likely that we are actually reading Peter's remembrances of the events surrounding Christ's life, ministry, and death as Mark recorded them. It is also likely that the young man fleeing from the garden in Mark 14:51 was actually Mark himself, for there would be no good reason to include that event if it were not his way of telling the reader that he himself was there.

- A strong restoration to service with Paul. In Paul's final letter he writes to Timothy. As he is anticipating death, he asks his son in the faith to come and visit with these words: "Only Luke is with me. Pick up Mark and bring him with you, for he is useful to me for service" (2 Timothy 4:11). The same John Mark whom Paul viewed as excess baggage some fifteen to twenty years earlier he now considered a valuable brother and co-worker in spiritual service. Why? Because Barnabas had not given up on John Mark!

◆

Barnabas was committed to being a builder—not of buildings, corporations, or empires, but of people. He took that which termites of criticism, discouragement, failure, and loss had been busy tearing down, repaired what had been broken, and then went on to build something even stronger by the grace of God. Barnabas's ministry of encouragement built an apostle, a great church, and a young giant for God. This is the testimony of Barnabas, the son of encouragement and a true spiritual carpenter.

We all need someone to be a Barnabas in our lives. In my life that person was Tobyann Davis.

As a college freshman I was required to take a first-semester speech class, a class in which Tobyann Davis was the instructor. I was an older student, entering college at twenty-one, but I was absolutely paralyzed with anxiety about getting up in front of people and talking. (Just for the record, I once saw a survey that said public speaking is the number one fear of Americans—death came in third.) I was terrified.

Our first assignment? Well, it seemed innocent enough. We had to give a sixty-second speech in which we introduced ourselves to the class. (At least I was moderately familiar with the subject matter.) I sat in the back of the classroom and dreaded the moment when Mrs. Davis would call my name. Finally that fateful moment arrived, and I stepped to the front of the class. I had barely gotten my name out when I panicked, bolted, and ran, in tears, from the classroom. My fear and anxiety so consumed me at the moment that it far outweighed any thought of what people would think of me. I only knew I had to get out of there. While my fellow students had a lot of fun riding me about my fears, Tobyann was different. She tracked me down and informed me that in the spring she would be producing the school drama and that I would be in it. I looked at her in disbelief. How could I stand before several thousand people when I couldn't handle the twenty kids in my freshman speech class? "You'll have one line. Only one line," she informed me. "And I'm going to work with you on that one line until you can do it perfectly."

For weeks we worked and worked . . . and worked. And the night of the performance, when the moment came for my one line—I nailed it! As soon as the words left my mouth, I looked at Tobyann, who was sitting in the front row. She had tears in her eyes and a huge smile on her face.

In the thirty years since then, I have been the pastor of three churches and have preached and taught the Bible all over the world. I often think of how different my life might have been if not for my Barnabas, who invested in a stammering fear-filled kid. I also think about what I hope will be a wonderful reward for Tobyann when she stands before the Savior, because her investment has made a difference in so many lives.

Carpenters and termites. Are you building or destroying? May God deliver us from those who, like termites, would destroy, and may He make of us an army of carpenters who can build one another up in the name of Christ for His own great glory! Whether they are named

Barnabas or Tobyann, I'm thankful for every person who is willing to make a difference by being an encourager to the hearts of other believers.

Principles from the Life of Barnabas

◆ A life is worth investing in, even though it may involve a risk.

◆ A life is worth investing in, even though it may result in disappointment.

◆ A life is worth investing in, because the impact can expand exponentially into other lives.

◆ A life is worth investing in, because it makes an impact upon eternity by impacting lives that will live forever somewhere.

3

Jezebel

A Corrupt Spirit

I had the privilege of growing up in a home where none of us doubted how Mom and Dad felt about each other. They had a love affair that never quit. They did everything together, from grocery shopping to cooking to housework to raising a house (literally) filled with seven children. So linked together were they that my mom never even had a driver's license until after my father passed away. Whenever she had to go anywhere, Dad took her. Their obvious love for each other survived parenting, challenging family relationships, a failed business endeavor, and weighty financial pressures. Late in his life, when my dad's health was failing and he would sometimes lose patience, one thing never changed—the look of love on his face whenever he looked at my mom.

This set the bar pretty high for me (and my siblings), and when I started looking for a woman with whom to build a marriage and a family, I had large expectations. Actually not large, enormous . . . gargantuan . . . colossal . . . maybe even unrealistic. My question was: Where could I find this paragon of feminine virtue? A Christian friend advised me, "If you want to find a rose, you don't look in the wilderness. You look in a rose garden." So I headed off to a Christian college as a twenty-one-year-old freshman with two priorities: find a wife and make the football team.

During my college years, I dated several wonderful young women. Yet not until I met one particular young woman did I encounter the one who, to my very demanding eye, might fulfill the image of a Proverbs 31 woman. Knowing I was going into ministry, I had at least some understanding that the demands, expectations, and pressures a pastor's wife might face could easily pound the life out of a genuine heart. But in my wife, Marlene, I found a woman who was all I could have hoped for—and more. We have been married for over twenty-five years, and through those years I have been told repeatedly that she is the quintessential pastoral partner. Her spirit and heart make her welcome in any and all situations, and her wisdom and character make her a powerful co-laborer. When I read the passages in Proverbs that talk about the character of a godly woman, I recognize that, more often than not, my wife lives out those wonderful truths.

But the book of Proverbs also describes another kind of woman:

The woman of folly is boisterous, she is naive and knows nothing (Proverbs 9:13).
As a ring of gold in a swine's snout so is a beautiful woman who lacks discretion (Proverbs 11:22).

An excellent wife is the crown of her husband, but she
who shames him is like rottenness in his bones (Proverbs 12:4).
It is better to live in a corner of a roof than in a house
shared with a contentious woman (Proverbs 21:9).
It is better to live in a desert land than with a contentious
and vexing woman (Proverbs 21:19).
A constant dripping on a day of steady rain and a contentious woman are alike (Proverbs 27:15).

It's hard to imagine one woman being so corrupt and
sinful as to embody all of these despicable traits. Yet that
woman did exist, and she lived out these evil and destructive traits, and more, to the fullest. That woman was Jezebel, and her corrupt spirit, like a twisted Midas touch,
marred and tainted everything she touched. She was not a
person to emulate or model, but she is definitely someone
who can teach us some significant lessons for life.

Concerns from Her Past

The power of a name is undeniable. A good name can
bear witness to a good heart. It can offer hope and peace.
This was certainly the case for Jim Dickenson.

A waist gunner on a bomber for the United States Army
Air Corps during World War II, Jim and his compatriots
were shot down during a bombing run over Nazi Germany. He survived the crash, only to be captured and spend
eighteen months in a German prisoner-of-war camp. For
the duration of his imprisonment, Jim and his fellow cap-
tives had little to feel good about, and even less cause for
hope. Yet, for reasons he could never explain, one thing in
that ugly place spoke to him of beauty and hope, and that

was a popular song, "Lili Marlene," that was frequently played over the camp speaker system to entertain the German guards. As Jim Dickenson listened, the melody of the music and the beauty of that name gave him a sense of hope that carried him through the trials of the camp and back home to America and his wife, Phyllis. When, some years later, Jim and Phyllis adopted a six-month-old baby girl, Jim saw in her all the promise that had pulled him through the months in the prison camp, and they named her Lili Marlene. Through the years, Lili Marlene lived up to her father's hopes and dreams, and was everything he could have ever longed for in a daughter. Jim told me all of this when I asked him for her hand in marriage!

A name can be a powerful thing. It can represent to us someone who is the embodiment of great hope and encouragement, but it can also remind us of someone who has brought us great disappointment and loss. Names are either a reflection of character or a mockery of it. Nowhere is that more evident than in the name Jezebel, which, according to Herbert Lockyer, originally meant "chaste, pure, free from carnal connections" (Lockyer, *All the Women of the Bible*, 73). Sadly, though, one bearer of this name was definitely not an example of truth in advertising. In fact, as we will see, her character was the polar opposite of the original meaning of her name. Like Judas, whose name meant "Jehovah is praised," her once-lovely name became so corrupted by her evil life that it is now the emblem of all that is unholy, evil, and perverse in womanhood. The name *Jezebel* stirs strong mental images and emotional reactions, and seldom are those responses positive.

The name of Jezebel's father, a significant element in understanding her family background, is worth noting as well. Notice what it says in 1 Kings 16:31: "It came about, as though it had been a trivial thing for him [Ahab] to walk in the sins of Jeroboam the son of Nebat, that he married Jezebel the daughter of Ethbaal king of the Sidonians, and went to serve Baal and worshiped him."

"Ethbaal," whose name means "man of Baal," was king of the Sidonians, residents of one of the twin Phoenician cities of Tyre and Sidon located in the coastal regions of Assyria just north of the Galilean area of Israel, the Northern Kingdom. In addition to being the king, Ethbaal also served as high priest of the Sidonians' pagan religion of Baal worship. John Whitcomb states that Ethbaal offered his daughter (Jezebel) in marriage to Ahab, son of Omri, as a political alliance, a strategy not uncommon in the ancient world. With the alliance secured by this marriage, Israel may have felt it was safe from a military action from Assyria; but in actuality it had become even more vulnerable to divine chastening. This vulnerability was rooted in the disobedience of Ahab in marrying Jezebel. Why?

- She was a non-Jew. God had commanded the Hebrew people not to intermarry with people from the surrounding Gentile nations, tribes, or people groups, largely to protect the nation from the infiltration of pagan religions.
- She was an unbeliever. It was not uncommon for people from the surrounding Gentile nations to convert to Judaism and embrace faith in the God of Abraham, Isaac, and Jacob. When Gentile women embraced the faith of Israel, Jewish men had the freedom to marry them. This was the case with Boaz and Ruth, whose

family line included David, king of Israel, and ultimately Christ Himself. Thus, far more significant than Jezebel's lack of Jewish blood was her lack of true faith.

- She was a pagan influence that would corrupt Israel. When King Solomon died, Jeroboam (son of Nebat, a servant of King Solomon) and Rehoboam (Solomon's son) divided the kingdom into a northern realm (Israel, headquartered in the city of Samaria) and a southern monarchy (Judah, whose capital was Jerusalem). Ahab, ruler of the northern kingdom, presided over a nation that had been spiritually and morally weakened by decades of battling against the siren song of idolatry—and losing.

As we begin to look closely at the passages that tell Jezebel's story, we see that the text strongly implies that she was extraordinarily beautiful. This beauty, however, masked a wicked heart. Though Jezebel was apparently beautiful and intelligent, with a strong personality and an even stronger will, she didn't have the character to channel those strengths for good. She prostituted all her good gifts to further evil. And that is key to understanding her story: talent, ability, appearance, power—all are meaningless apart from a heart for God, and will eventually be corrupted.

Notice how that corruption is seen in her life.

Issues in Jezebel's Life

RELIGION WITHOUT GOD

Satan's primary goal from the beginning has been to lead people to worship and serve anything or anyone *except* the true and living God. Our spiritual enemy doesn't care who or what we worship—he doesn't even care if we worship him; he just doesn't want us to worship the living God. Notice, for example, in the story of Job, that Satan's goal was not to turn Job into a devil-worshiper. The spiritual enemy's only goal was to drive Job into cursing and rejecting God. Very little has changed since the days of Job. It doesn't matter if it is the worship of something intangible (like fame, power, ideology, or success) or something tangible (like money, material possessions, or actual idols). Worship of anything other than God allows that thing or person to fill the role of God in your life. This religion without God is a one-way road to disappointment now and destruction later.

Several years ago I was invited to teach at a Bible institute in Togo, West Africa, training pastors for the growing evangelical church in that country. As we traveled to a distant village church for a ministry opportunity, we drove through several other villages. As we passed through one of these communities, our missionary-host commented, "This village has had a bad year." This particular village didn't look any better or worse than the dozen other villages we had seen, so I asked him how he knew that. He pointed to a collapsed thatched roof shelter and said, "Under that debris is a pile of mud, which is the village god. The people of the village are angry at their god, and as a result have not repaired its house. They must have had a bad year to be so angry at their god."

In the West we might find such a notion of a "pile-of-mud god" humorous, but it really isn't funny at all. Following any god but the true and living God is a spiritual slavery that offers no hope of escape. It is the consequence of a sincere, even fervent, pursuit of false religion, and it ends in an empty idolatry, no matter what form that idol might take.

For Jezebel, it was Baal worship, a ruthless religion whose god required torture, human sacrifice, and ritual prostitution. And Jezebel was not content to hold that religion as her own. She brought this idolatry into her marriage, her home, and, as the wife of a king, to her nation. Look at 1 Kings 16:31–34:

> And it came about, as though it had been a trivial thing for him to walk in the sins of Jeroboam the son of Nebat, that he [Ahab] married Jezebel the daughter of Ethbaal king of the Sidonians, and went to serve Baal and worshiped him. So he [Ahab] erected an altar for Baal in the house of Baal which he built in Samaria. Ahab also made the Asherah. Thus Ahab did more to provoke the Lord God of Israel than all the kings of Israel who were before him. In his days Hiel the Bethelite built Jericho; he laid its foundations with the loss of Abiram his first-born, and set up its gates with the loss of his youngest son Segub, according to the word of the Lord, which He spoke by Joshua the son of Nun.

Through her powerful influence over her husband Ahab, king of the northern kingdom of Israel, Jezebel caused idols

- to be built in Ahab's house.
- to be housed in the temple built at Jezreel, and to have those idols serviced by more than 400 priests.
- to be housed in the temple built at Samaria, and to be serviced by another 450 priests.

- to be the focus of Israel's worship. (She attempted to drive out the prophets of God [1 Kings 18:4] and to exterminate the worship of the God of Israel.)
- to be paramount in the minds of the people. (Jezebel's goal was to eradicate the worship of Jehovah, even after blatant defeat at the hands of the true God of Israel and His servant Elijah on Mount Carmel.)

Few things are so genuinely tragic as a person totally committed to the wrong thing. We have seen this in our own culture in the disastrous examples of Jim Jones and the People's Temple, the tragedy of the Heaven's Gate cult, and the fiery end of the Branch Davidian cult in Waco, Texas. These people were committed to their beliefs, even to the point of death. That was Jezebel. She did not lack commitment, but she was deeply and intensely committed to the wrong god.

RULING OVER AHAB

Jezebel dominated Ahab and every aspect of his life. Notice what the Old Testament says about the hold she had over her husband, the king of Israel:

- She controlled his worship: "It came about, as though it had been a trivial thing for him to walk in the sins of Jeroboam the son of Nebat, that he married Jezebel the daughter of Ethbaal king of the Sidonians, and went to serve Baal and worshiped him" (1 Kings 16:31).
- She controlled his leadership: "Now Ahab told Jezebel all that Elijah had done, and how he had killed all the prophets with the sword. Then Jezebel sent a

messenger to Elijah, saying, 'So may the gods do to me and even more, if I do not make your life as the life of one of them by tomorrow about this time'" (1 Kings 19:1–2).

- She controlled his thinking: "Surely there was no one like Ahab who sold himself to do evil in the sight of the Lord, because Jezebel his wife incited him" (1 Kings 21:25).

This is exactly the kind of dominant, destructive wife the writers of the Proverbs warned about. Jezebel was a tremendous burden to her husband, no matter how beautiful she might be. Instead of coming alongside him as a marriage partner and supportive wife, she sought to rule over her husband, and, as a result, through him to rule over Israel.

How differently life plays out when a wife is a supportive partner to her husband instead of a dominating controller, and when a husband encourages his wife's pursuit of excellence. It has been said that behind every successful man is a good woman and a surprised mother-in-law. The fact, however, is that we are impacted greatly by our life-partners. Our successes can be enhanced by their support and involvement, and our failures can be aggravated by their lack of compassion and stinging words. The role of a partner can be painful and challenging, but a strong commitment to a true, shared partnership makes all the difference in how we run the race before us. Not rulership or, at the other extreme, slavery, but *partnership*. Unfortunately for both Ahab and Jezebel, neither of them learned this priceless lesson.

HEARTLESS REVENGE

In 1 Kings 19:1–2, Jezebel takes off both the gloves and her mask: "Now Ahab told Jezebel all that Elijah had done, and how he had killed all the prophets with the sword. Then Jezebel sent a messenger to Elijah, saying, 'So may the gods do to me and even more, if I do not make your life as the life of one of them by tomorrow about this time.'"

Behind Jezebel's mask of beauty was a woman filled with hate, bitterness, and desire for revenge. And when the mask came off, that ugly reality was revealed. In the spirit of a fair competition, you could say that on Mount Carmel the rules were set, agreed to, and followed—and the best man (or, in this case, deity) won. Jezebel was not much of a "live and let live" sort of person, however. She heard the reports of the Baal priests' failure—and subsequent execution—and determined that she would make it her life's mission to see Elijah (the human burr under her saddle) hacked into pieces just as those false priests had been!

Jezebel's goal was not justice or fair play. It was an expression of the darkness of her heart—a heart cut so deeply by the failure of the Baal priests on Carmel that she could think of nothing but a bloody death for her adversary, Elijah. She was a miserable person, and she made everyone around her miserable. She had the same twisted heart that centuries later would be displayed in Herodias, who so desperately desired the death of John the Baptist that she was willing to prostitute her daughter to pressure Herod into executing the prophet who had confronted her adultery.

It has been said that revenge is a dish that is best served cold, but revenge is never "best." Cold or hot, revenge is a bitter and lonely way to live, and it often coexists with another tragic practice.

RELENTLESS SELF-WILL

In 1 Kings 21:1–25 we see how Jezebel's corrupt spirit expressed itself in several particularly brutal ways. But along with its brutality, this is also a pathetic picture. A man named Naboth owned a vineyard that abutted King Ahab's palace in Samaria. Apparently it was a rich and productive garden area that Naboth had worked and developed. We aren't given an abundance of details about it, but to Naboth the agricultural value of the land, high as it was, was overshadowed by the emotional and family attachment he had to it. Ahab coveted this land and asked to have it, but Naboth responded to Ahab's overtures with a flat no: "The Lord forbid me that I should give you the inheritance of my fathers" (1 Kings 21:3). It was a matter of family allegiance mingled with spiritual commitment— two concepts totally foreign to Ahab.

A measured and mature response to Naboth's rejection would have been the response worthy of a king. Unfortunately, Ahab responded like a pampered child. "So Ahab went into his house sullen and displeased because of the word which Naboth the Jezreelite had spoken to him; for he had said, 'I will not give you the inheritance of my fathers.' And he lay down on his bed, and turned away his face, and would eat no food" (v. 4 NKJV).

Once again Jezebel steps in to take the lead. While Ahab mopes and sulks, she takes over and acts out of her own self-will. With no regard for the rights or property of others, and with no respect for her childish husband, Jezebel takes matters into her own hands in a series of actions that are intended to get Ahab his vineyard while cementing her own position of power in the kingdom. Included are:

- Mockery: "But Jezebel his wife came to him [Ahab], and said to him, 'Why is your spirit so sullen that you eat no food?' So he said to her, 'Because I spoke to Naboth the Jezreelite, and said to him, "Give me your vineyard for money; or else, if it pleases you, I will give you another vineyard for it." And he answered, "I will not give you my vineyard."' Then Jezebel his wife said to him, 'You now exercise authority over Israel! Arise and eat food, and let your heart be cheerful; I will give you the vineyard of Naboth the Jezreelite'" (1 Kings 21:5–7 NKJV).

She mocked her husband and ridiculed his childish response to not getting his way. She had no intention of being ridiculed by Ahab's weakness, and was determined to take care of the matter.

- Manipulation: It is clear from verse 7 that Jezebel was the real power behind the throne. She understood power and how to use it to get what she wanted. She also knew how to maneuver her husband to make use of his power in achieving her goals.
- Murder: Jezebel was willing to do whatever was needed to maintain power. "So she wrote letters in Ahab's name, sealed them with his seal, and sent the letters to the elders and the nobles who were dwelling in the city with Naboth. And she wrote in

the letters, saying, 'Proclaim a fast, and seat Naboth with high honor among the people; and seat two men, scoundrels, before him to bear witness against him, saying, "You have blasphemed God and the king." Then take him out, and stone him, that he may die'" (1 Kings 21:8–10 NKJV).

The strategies of a corrupt heart know no limit. The corrupt heart is willing to do anything and everything necessary to achieve personal desires, and that willingness is unrestrained by scruples, morals, or human values. Most of all, the corrupt heart is untouched and unfazed by mercy, compassion, or care. It is, at the end of the day, determined to advance personal longings at all costs.

The destructive nature of a heart without God cannot be overstated. For Jezebel, a passion for power and control (not always one and the same) drove her to a tragic life with even more tragic results. She was willing to decimate any and all in the pursuit of her own desires. Her frighteningly utilitarian perspective on life allowed her to become proficient in "Loving things and using people" (B. J. Thomas). Ultimately, her blind devotion to her pagan gods caused her to destroy all that she should have loved.

The Legacy of Her Life

Outside the "Haunted Mansion" attraction at Disneyland is a "comic" cemetery, where the tombstones tell the stories of fictitious people not buried there. My favorite epitaph is, "Here lies Lester Moore, / Two shots from a .44, / No less no more, / No Les no more." In the real world, we tend, with even less cleverness, to minimize the impact of individual lives. A long and fruitful life is reduced to a few lines on a three-by-five obituary card handed by the funeral director to the officiating pastor just before the funeral service.

For some reason, in today's world we struggle to embrace a sense of legacy in the lives and deaths of those around us. Legacy seems to be something reserved for the rich, famous, and powerful, as though these "legends in their own time" (or "in their own mind") are sole proprietors of such significance. The truth is, every life leaves a legacy. Each life creates a ripple in the pond that impacts the lives of others—perhaps many lives, perhaps few, but other lives nonetheless. Even Jezebel had a legacy, albeit a singularly ugly one.

In the end, God pronounced judgment upon this corrupt and depraved woman with these powerful words:

> And concerning Jezebel the LORD also spoke, saying, "The dogs shall eat Jezebel by the wall of Jezreel. The dogs shall eat whoever belongs to Ahab and dies in the city, and the birds of the air shall eat whoever dies in the field." But there was no one like Ahab who sold himself to do wickedness in the sight of the LORD, because Jezebel his wife stirred him up. And he behaved very abominably in following idols, according to all that the Amorites had done, whom the LORD had cast out before the children of Israel (1 Kings 21:23–26 NKJV).

Jezebel thoroughly deserved this judgment, and her death is one of the most gruesome events depicted in Scripture. But God does not delight in such judgment. "I have no pleasure in the death of the wicked, but that the wicked turn from his way and live. Turn, turn from your evil ways!

For why should you die, O house of Israel?" (Ezekiel 33:11 NKJV). God's desire is for those committed to wrongdoing to turn away from their sin and live.

Defiantly, Jezebel painted her face and styled her hair, determined to prepare herself externally for death (2 Kings 9:30 ff.). Sadly, she saw no need to prepare her soul. She reaped what she had sown in violence and bloodshed, and, unrepentant to the end, plunged into eternity without God. Jezebel was cast out of an upstairs window, apparently by two of her own servants, splattering the walls of the building with her blood. Her body was then crushed under horses' hooves until the remains were left to be eaten by the scavenging street dogs. A dark ending for a dark heart.

Lessons from Her Example

Jezebel lived hundreds of years before Christ, but she was not soon forgotten. In fact, she became an Old Testament picture of a New Testament truth. In Revelation 2–3, John tells of letters that the Lord Jesus Christ sent to seven churches in Asia Minor—letters designed to offer encouragement, correction, and challenge to the first-century believers that made up those assemblies. In Christ's letter to the church at Thyatira, He warned them of the danger of false teachers leading the church into spiritual adultery (Revelation 2:18–19).

To visualize this danger, Jesus said:

> "Nevertheless I have a few things against you, because you allow that woman Jezebel, who calls herself a prophetess, to teach and beguile My servants to commit sexual immorality and to eat things sacrificed to idols. And I gave her time

to repent of her sexual immorality, and she did not repent. Indeed I will cast her into a sickbed, and those who commit adultery with her into great tribulation, unless they repent of their deeds" (Revelation 2:20–22 NKJV).

The church at Thyatira was endangered by a false teacher who, like Jezebel of old, would be a corrupter of God's people. Like Jezebel, this false teacher, if choosing to refuse repentance, would most certainly receive judgment.

Legacies do not come by accident; they result from choices. Those who choose to follow Jezebel's destructive example—either men or women—will leave a decidedly different legacy than those who live out the godly character traits described in Proverbs 31. The choices we make will determine the legacy we leave behind.

Part of a godly legacy is that a woman's children will "rise up and call her blessed" (Proverbs 31:28 NKJV). Unfortunately that was a legacy that eluded Jezebel. But it remains a legacy available to the person who is willing to make the right choices for the right reasons.

As I write this, my wife is showing our youngest son, Mark, how to form basic chords on a thirty-year-old acoustic guitar. As she helps him in his efforts to make his fingers move from a C-chord to an F-chord, she is not thinking about a "mother of the year award." Her only desire is to invest in Mark's life because she loves him. This is time she could spend a hundred different ways, but she has made a strategic choice to sit and teach a twelve-year-old how to play the guitar. In the eyes of a world preoccupied with its own definition of greatness, it is a waste of time. In the heart of a child, it is a moment that may become a memory, and a memory that could become a talent, and a talent that might become a reality, and a reality that could define a legacy. It is a legacy born of little moments—moments given life by important choices that the world never sees.

Principles from the Life of Jezebel

Jezebel is a human danger sign who warns us of:

◆ The great danger of choosing the wrong god to worship and serve with your life, no matter how sincere and fervent that choice might be.

◆ The great danger in a life of manipulation that chooses to gain from personal desires at the expense of others.

◆ The great danger in allowing ourselves to relish revenge and cherish hatred—danger not only to others, but to our own hearts as well.

◆ The great danger in promoting the physical and ignoring the spiritual, pursuing the temporal and ignoring the eternal, and promoting self-interest and ignoring the needs of others.

4

Jochebed

A Notable Mom

During my years as a pastor, few of the so-called "special days" in the church's annual calendar were as truly special as Mother's Day. We would recognize the newest mom in the service that day, as well as the "most experienced" (politically correct language for the oldest) and the mother with the most children (an award my mom won for seven straight years). Why all the hoopla? Why the red and white carnations on Mother's Day? Why the special meals and cards and gifts? Why is it that the phone lines are more congested on Mother's Day than any other day of the year? Because mothers are special people.

Nothing, or no one, in life draws from our hearts the emotion and connectedness we have with our mothers. Some interesting snapshots of life confirm this. The 300-pound professional NFL football players who see the red light of the television camera and yell out, "Hi Mom!" The young musician who completes her recital piece, then searches the crowd eagerly for one face that matters above all—her mother. The soldiers returning from combat zones who find comfort and home by weeping on the sometimes bent, sometimes weary, but always strong-enough shoulders of their mothers. The college sophomore in the stands of a televised college basketball game who holds up a hand-lettered sign that says, "Hi Mom! Send money!" (Okay, so that one is not so great.)

Still, the special relationship a mother has with her children is seen in the devotion, impact, and influence she lavishes on those young lives. It is evidenced in a mother's ability to see what no one else sees when she looks at her precious child. A mother's heart is a heart of hope, optimism, confidence, and unwavering love. It is not a heart that is deceived or deluded, but a heart that sees and celebrates all that her child can be.

During World War I (1914–1918) a soldier named Jim marched through an entire military parade out of step with the other soldiers in his troop. As the troops marched by—perfectly synchronized except for poor Jim—his mother had a very different perspective. She wondered aloud, "Why is everyone out of step but Jim?" Misguided though she was, she believed completely in her boy.

An aged, white-haired mother sat with a smile on her face, waiting for her famous son, former Supreme Allied Commander during World War II and soon-to-be president of the United States, Dwight David Eisenhower. Someone said to her, "You must be proud of your great and illustrious son." To which she replied, "Which son?" (She had seven sons.)

69

Napoleon Bonaparte said, "The future destiny of a child is the work of a mother." That seems to be perfectly pictured by Susanna Wesley. She was the mother of nineteen children, including two who became the spiritual leaders of the Great Awakening, John and Charles Wesley. Susanna influenced her children even in the reading they selected, and shaped their lives with profound spiritual guidance.

A mother's role and influence are undeniably significant. Another woman whose life is testimony to this is Jochebed. Her impact on the lives of her children shook and shaped the world of her day with a force that ripples even to the world of our day. Such is the power of a godly mother.

An Anonymous Past

For someone whose influence was so far-reaching, Jochebed seems to have come to a place of impact out of utter anonymity. Though we see her in action at times when she remains unnamed, we see her name recorded only twice in the Old Testament. "Amram married his father's sister Jochebed, and she bore him Aaron and Moses. . . . The name of Amram's wife was Jochebed, the daughter of Levi, who was born to Levi in Egypt; and she bore to Amram: Aaron and Moses and their sister Miriam" (Exodus 6:20; Numbers 26:59). But what a great name she bore, for *Jochebed* means "Jehovah is her glory."

What is interesting about Jochebed's name is that she seems to be the first person in the Old Testament to have a name compounded from the name *Jehovah* (*Jah*), though there had been others with names compounded from *El* (*Elohim*). The name *Jehovah* appears in the Old Testament record in Genesis 2:4, but was apparently not well-known until Moses wrote the Pentateuch (the first five books of the Bible). Had *Jehovah* been a well-known name for God prior to the burning bush, there would have been a record of compound names based on that divine name. Many early names were compounded from the name *El* (or *Elohim*), and the practice would likely have been extended to other known names for God. It is possible, however, that Moses gave this name to his mother years later as a testimony to her godly character.

The rest of Jochebed's family had a quiet consequence as well. Amram, her husband, was a descendant of Levi, the head of the priestly tribe of the nation of Israel. Amram was also Jochebed's nephew. This sounds strange in our culture, where marriages between family members is not considered "socially acceptable," but such inter-family marriages were common in those days. After the establishment of the Mosaic law, limitations were placed on marriages between family members. Nevertheless, the marriage of Amram and his aunt, Jochebed, produced at least three children—children who had a powerful impact on their world, and ours:

- Aaron was Israel's first high priest and the beginning of the Aaronic priesthood. He was Moses' primary aide and confidant, was set apart by God to be the spokesman for Moses, and was instrumental in establishing the practices of the ceremonial sacrificial system of Israel. Aaron had his own episodes of failure, but nonetheless he was a significant character in the formation of the early nation of Israel.

- Miriam was a gifted poetess and musician. She was intimately associated with her brothers in leading Israel, and was looked to as a leader in her own right. (Read more about her in chapter 7.)

- Moses was one of the greatest national and spiritual leaders the world has ever known, leading Israel out of slavery in Egypt to the very cusp of the Promised Land of Canaan. His relationship with the living God was profound and personal, so much so that "the Lord used to speak to Moses face to face, just as a man speaks to his friend" (Exodus 33:11). Although Moses' character was flawed by episodes of anger, this dynamic man was also described as "more [humble] than anyone" (Numbers 12:3 NIV).

God chose three of Jochebed's children to lead His people from slavery to freedom, from tribal diversity to national integrity, and from a land of bondage to the land of promise. The godliness of her children and the range of their achievements are a credit to her, and the impact of her spiritual legacy will be measured only in eternity, when we have the benefit of perfect hindsight.

An Act of Courage

Exodus 2:1–10 is the only place in Scripture where Jochebed steps onto center stage. Yet we can learn much from her singular moment in the spotlight. The stage setting for this event stretches back some four hundred years to the time when Joseph, who had risen to prominence as Pharaoh's commander-in-chief, moved his father and his eleven brothers and their families to Egypt to save them from the devastation of a worldwide famine. In Egypt, under Pharaoh's protection, the children of Israel prospered, grew, multiplied, and became a great, extended tribal family. But over four hundred years later their condition of life changed dramatically! The situation is described in a brilliant economy of words in Exodus 1.

- A new king (1:8). When Joseph was God's instrument of rescue for Egypt, his name and family received the honor and gratitude of the nation for generations to come. Unfortunately, all good things must come to an end. And when a pharaoh who had little interest in ancient history rose to power, things changed dramatically. He was not concerned with what had happened hundreds of years before; what was past was past. All he saw was the major presence of foreigners in his land—a presence that could be an internal threat to the nation.

This occurs regularly in human history, as past allies become present foes. Often it doesn't even take hundreds of years; sometimes it happens in the blink of the eye. In November of 1979, for example, after years of close alliance between Iran and the United States, in a blur of chaos and terror under a new Iranian regime, our embassy in Tehran was overrun and the embassy personnel were kidnapped and held captive for 444 days. With unbelievable swiftness, a former ally became an enemy. With the rise of the Ayatollah Khomeni, the cooperation of the past was forgotten, just as it was when a new pharaoh arose "who did not know Joseph."

- New conditions (1:9–10). The Hebrew people had prospered in the Goshen province of Egypt. They had grown in numbers and grown in resources. Suddenly their neighbors viewed them as a "fifth column"—an enemy within.
- Bonds of slavery (1:11–13). To combat this perceived internal danger, the pharaoh ordered the Israelites enslaved. He turned them into an economic boon for the nation and a pauperized work force, subject to torture, beatings, and death if they disobeyed their taskmasters.
- Genocide (1:14–16). Still, the massive presence of the Hebrew people within their borders remained a threat in the eyes of the Egyptians. To stunt the growth of this family-nation, the government ordered the death of all newborn Hebrew sons.

HER COURAGE (2:2)

Jochebed was undaunted by this decree. Because she valued the life of her own precious infant son more than she valued her own, she defied the king's command and hid the child instead of killing him. The letter of Hebrews, in the wonderful "Hall of Faith" passage found in chapter 11, describes her motivation this way: "By faith Moses, when he was born, was hidden for three months by his parents, because they saw he was a beautiful child; and they were not afraid of the king's edict" (Hebrews 11:23).

74

Along with Amram, her husband, Jochebed believed God more than she feared the king! This is biblical civil disobedience. True civil disobedience operates out of conscience, not convenience. It stands on deeply held principles and readily accepts the consequences of those principled choices.

Having grown up in the 1960s, I remember the Vietnam War protests all too clearly. I remember those who opposed the war, even to the point of the destruction of property, or worse. Yet there was a missing element to many of the protests, and that was the willingness to accept the potential consequences of their stand. One notable exception was Muhammad Ali (formerly Cassius Clay). Rather than serve in the military, he protested as a conscientious objector—and stood firm. But instead of fleeing to Canada or some other safe haven, at the height of his career—the greatest boxing career the sport has ever seen—he submitted to the law and served the required jail time.

Similarly, Amram and Jochebed recognized and accepted the cost they might pay for their refusal to bow to authority. Even so, they hid their baby boy—and, believe me, this is not an easy task. As I write this, I am sitting on an airplane on my way to Perth, Australia, and in the seat behind me is an infant. How can such a small set of lungs produce such ear-piercing sounds? (And by the way, as the father of five children I had learned this lesson long before I got on this particular flight.) How do you hide a three-month-old infant, especially in a culture of open houses? In that day, homes were basically one room with open windows. Not exactly a secure environment. But Jochebed and her husband made it secure enough to protect the child's life, despite the fact that discovery would have meant certain death for them and their child, and perhaps even the rest of their family.

Let's put this in perspective: Contrast Jochebed's willingness to sacrifice her life out of love for her child to the modern-day abortion advocates who, all too often, are willing to sacrifice the life of a child out of nothing more than personal convenience. A career, a love life, financial cost—all are deemed of greater value than a human soul. The killing of the Hebrew children would cost Egypt dearly, just as abortion is robbing our nation. We are in the process of losing an entire generation of young people and their potential contribution to our culture because of abortion. The United States is founded on the principles of the right to life, liberty, and the pursuit of happiness. What can never be assumed, however, is that my right to pursue happiness trumps another person's right to life. Sacrifice has been replaced by self-determination.

When I think of Jochebed's courageous act and her potentially great sacrifice, I also think of the Avenue of the Righteous among the Nations, which is the entryway to Yad Vashem, the Holocaust Memorial in Jerusalem. As you walk down this avenue, you walk between rows of trees planted in memory of those in Europe who risked their lives to rescue Jews from the camps, gas chambers, and ovens of Nazism. Before each tree is a plaque of remembrance engraved with names that should never be forgotten: Oskar Schindler, Corrie ten Boom, and many others. People who saw life as something to be protected, not something to be cast onto the rubbish heap.

There was a great sense of priority in Jochebed's desire to rescue her child from death. It was not a matter of convenience or comfort. It was the significance of a life bearing the image of God. Besides that, she had a great sense of love and responsibility for the life of this child—her child.

HER SPIRITUAL SENSITIVITY (2:2)

Along with her courage and desire to save her child, Jochebed also had the spiritual sensitivity to recognize that there was something special about her baby, some special purpose for which he had been born, causing her to work even harder to protect him. Notice the way this is described years later by Moses himself, as well as in two New Testament books:

- The woman [Jochebed] conceived and bore a son; and when she saw that he was beautiful, she hid him (Exodus 2:2).
- It was at this time that Moses was born; and he was lovely in the sight of God (Acts 7:20).
- By faith Moses, when he was born, was hidden for three months by his parents, because they saw he was a beautiful child; and they were not afraid of the king's edict (Hebrews 11:23).

Of these three statements, the one that is most interesting to me is Acts 7:20. *Beautiful* means "fair in the eyes of God." This doesn't speak of mere physical attractiveness, but of this child being special, unique, even set apart for God.

Jochebed seems to have been sensitive to this uniqueness in her child, just as we need to be sensitive to the uniqueness of our children. We need to look at the destiny, providence, and untold promise in every little child. Jesus showed just such tenderness and concern for children, reflected in His wonderful words, "Let the little children come to Me, and do not forbid them; for of such is the kingdom of heaven" (Matthew 19:14 NKJV). A serious commitment to impacting the lives of children—whether our own children, or children whose hearts have been entrusted to us in ministry—is not easy, and it is often uncomfortable, and sometimes things don't go smoothly. Nevertheless, our children deserve our spiritual concern, and the benefits for doing it will be seen for generations to come. In the relay race that is life, we are preparing our children to receive the baton so that they can run the race after us.

God can change the world through a single life. Look at the difference Jochebed made in her world because of her commitment to the life of just one child!

HER INGENUITY (2:3)

A dilemma has been described as a situation where either a yes or no answer is wrong. In the classic dilemma, the question asked of a husband is, "Honey, does this dress make me look fat?" He had better be very careful how he answers.

But Jochebed faced a much more serious dilemma. If she obeyed the royal edict, her child died; if she disobeyed, she and her family might die. Throughout history, people have not defied royal imperatives unless it was an issue they were willing to die for. Jochebed apparently was. So faced with a life-or-death situation she had to come up with a creative alternative that would spare the life of her young son. And she did. Her idea was ingenious and has intrigued both serious students of Scripture and Sunday school children ever since.

- She wove a little watertight basket (a miniature ark) from the reeds that grew along the Nile. The NIV study notes say that the Hebrew word here for the *basket* or *ark* actually has Egyptian origin and is used only here and of Noah's ark (Genesis 6:14). Since these are both found in the historical records written by Moses it is interesting that he uses the same word in both places. A vessel for rescue and safety was prepared to deliver the child from certain death.
- She placed the baby in the little vessel and took it to the river at just the right time.
- She anticipated that the baby would be found.
- She left her daughter Miriam to watch and see what happened to the baby. (For Miriam's side of the story, see chapter 7.)

Sometimes it seems we have forgotten how to think creatively to find sound, proper, and beneficial alternatives to the challenges we face in life. Instead, we go with our first impression and allow ourselves to be driven by our feelings and emotions. Life experience teaches us, however, that firing from the hip usually results in greater problems instead of solutions. We learn this from our Lord Himself, for Jesus was, in addition to everything else, a master at the creative solution.

When the religious leaders of His day tried to trap Jesus, they did so by trying to catch Him on the horns of a dilemma. They presented Him with a woman caught in the act of adultery and demanded that He pronounce judgment on her (John 8). They thought they were leaving Christ with only two options: have her put to death by stoning (disregarding the law of love and upholding the law of Moses), or set her free (disregarding Moses' law and upholding the law of love). But faced with this dilemma, Jesus presented a third option: let the person among them who had no sin throw the first stone. In doing this, He upheld both the law of love and the law of Moses, and the woman's life was spared. This is the kind of creative thinking that looks beyond the dilemma of the moment and fashions the opportunity of the third option.

Jochebed, too, was a third-option kind of woman. Her creative thinking saved her son and her family—and resulted in placing her son in a position from which, ultimately, he could save a nation.

HER REWARD (2:9)

Pharaoh's daughter, who had come down to the Nile to bathe, found the baby and recognized him as a Hebrew child. Miriam, who had been watching nearby, asked the princess if she would like one of the Hebrew women to nurse the baby for her. Another instance of creative thinking! Thus, the daughter of the king adopted Moses as her own son, but Jochebed was always nearby, able to nurse and nurture her own baby, blessed with the opportunity to shape the life of her son.

Imagine this woman, nursing her own child, singing him the songs of Israel, and telling him the stories of the God of Abraham, Isaac, and Jacob—right in Pharaoh's palace! Imagine her pouring her love, her life, and her heart into his young mind and life. The day inevitably came when Moses was too old to require a nursemaid and was taken from her. He entered into palace life and was trained in the ways of Egypt. But Jochebed's early influence on her son paid dividends she never could have foreseen. "By faith Moses, when he had grown up, refused to be called the son of Pharaoh's daughter" (Hebrews 11:24).

Despite all the glory and wealth his adoption into the Egyptian royal family offered him, Moses would not reject his people or his family or his destiny! Why? I strongly believe that it was his mother's influence that had helped build his character from earliest childhood. Because Jochebed stood firmly upon God's principles, her son Moses learned to do so as well.

A Model of Faith

Like the ancient patriarch Job, Jochebed lived by faith. This is the point of Hebrews 11:23. "By faith" she trusted God in the midst of great danger and terrifying heartache, and the results of her faith changed her world. God's instrument for the rescue of Israel may have been Moses, but His instrument for the rescue of the rescuer was his mother. What a pattern she sets for us!

- Conviction. Jochebed's priorities were the protection, care, and training of her child. And her priorities were driven by conviction rather than convenience, by self-sacrifice rather than self-preservation, and were the result of sacrificial love and godly character.

81

- Creativity. Instead of taking the path of least resistance, instead of looking for the easy way out, Jochebed acted with thought and deliberation. As a result, she devised a creative alternative, and the danger of the situation was transformed into advantage.

- Confidence. Jochebed trusted God more than she feared Pharaoh. The strength of her faith conquered her fear. And it is not an overstatement to say that her faith and her resulting choices have impacted the life of virtually every person since. Just think of how different the world might have been had Moses not been safely delivered from Pharaoh's decree: no deliverance of Israel, no Sinai law-giving, no King David, very little if any Old Testament literature. Everything touched by the post-Egypt history of the nation of Israel carries with it the fingerprints of Jochebed—a third-option woman.

◆

Jochebed's name says it all: "Jehovah is her glory"! What a joy it must have been to have her beloved son, Moses, rise up and call her blessed. That is a testimony to envy and desire. Centuries later, the writer of Proverbs might have been thinking of her when he wrote: "Many daughters have done nobly, but you excel them all. Charm is deceitful and beauty is vain, but a woman who fears the Lord, she shall be praised" (Proverbs 31:29–30).

And 3,500 years later we still celebrate the legacy of Jochebed's faith. What a notable mom!

PRINCIPLES FROM THE LIFE OF JOCHEBED

◆ The Principle of Perseverance. The easy way is seldom the best or most meaningful way. Through willingness to take the road less traveled and the faithfulness to endure to the end, we have the opportunity to make a difference in our world.

◆ The Principle of Dependence. Life offers challenges that require us to look beyond ourselves and our own cleverness and abilities. But in the midst of those challenges we can depend upon the grace of God and trust Him with our futures and our families.

◆ The Principle of Consequence. When forced to the point of decision, we must be prepared to accept the consequences that may come. This is the reality of life in a fallen world, where good and right are often punished. The commitment to do right must not be contingent upon an expectation that the world will celebrate us. In most cases it will not.

◆ The Principle of Furtherance. If our values and convictions are to outlive us, we must invest in young hearts and lives with the spiritual truth and passion. As they embrace faith in Him and mature in that faith, our hearts may well be enriched by seeing the gospel go further through them than it ever could through us.

5

Lydia

A Career Woman

In the 1980s a popular television ad for Enjoli perfume had a young, energetic woman singing and acting out the edgy, driving lyrics: "I can bring home the bacon, fry it up in a pan, and never, ever let you forget you're a man. I'm a woman—Enjoli." This multi-million-dollar marketing plan portraying a new dawn of feminine independence seemed to echo Helen Reddy's hit single of the 1970s which had become the hymn of the new, independent woman: "I am strong / I am invincible / I am woman."

Similar rallying cries have emanated from women's groups at various points in recent history, calling for such things as women's suffrage, the passage of the Equal Rights Amendment, and equal pay for equal work. "Let women be all they can be," they cry. Many of these are legitimate issues that deserve careful thought, discussion, and resolution. Yet some of the debate seems to be more about creating the illusion of feminine strength than about offering actual opportunities for women to become strong contributors to our society.

In the midst of the hyperbole and rhetoric of the current gender debates, and the political and social hot potato this issue has become in today's world, we tend to believe that ours is the first era to wrestle seriously with the issues of women's rights and opportunities. Yet the idea of strong women making their way in the world is not unique to our time. As far back as the Old Testament and on into the New, the pages of the Bible picture wise, competent, and successful women who lived hundreds, even thousands, of years before the controversies of our allegedly sophisticated age. From Deborah, who led her people to war in the days of the judges (approximately 1250–1200 BC), to Priscilla, who trained Apollos (one of the early church's greatest preachers) in about AD 50–51, strong, independent women are part of the biblical landscape. And 2,000 years ago, Lydia of Philippi was setting a profound example for career women of all ages to follow!

A Life with a Foundation

Every person has a story. In our world of information overload, however, we often know far more about other people than we could have ever imagined—and in some cases, far more than we wish we knew. Frankly, do we need to know how many Botox injections the popular sitcom actress has had, or how many times a famous musician has endured a broken relationship? At the same time, think of the individuals you wish you could know better, or more personally. For me, one such person is Amelia Earhart. She was, as the Panasonic ads used to say, "Just slightly ahead of her time." In a day when women were largely relegated to the kitchen, she was a spirited pilot who was out to change the perception of women in the world. Her life has been well chronicled on film and on the printed page, yet a certain air of mystery surrounds her because of her untimely and mysterious death. There are huge holes in the information we have about her—her motives, her plans for the future, her relationships, even her ultimate goals. All of which only makes me more curious about what really happened to her.

In some ways, Lydia is the Amelia Earhart of the Bible. For a woman who seems to have had such prominence and to have been so dramatically beyond her times by becoming a career woman in such a male-dominated world, we have very little information about her. She, too, is surrounded by mystery, and no matter how much "inquiring minds [like mine] want to know," Lydia makes only a brief appearance on the stage of Scripture.

From the information and even the hints that we do find in a few verses in the book of Acts, however, we can deduce some interesting things about this first-century "Renaissance woman." A place to begin, as we now know is so often true, is with her name. The name *Lydia* means "bending" and is derived from the name of the country in which she lived. In fact, some Bible scholars say the reference to her should be translated generically as "the Lydian woman" instead of as a proper name, and that her true name is unknown. Though that may be true, for our purposes we will follow tradition and call her by name.

Lydia was from the city of Thyatira in the Lydia province of Asia Minor (modern Turkey). This province was the richest and most prosperous country in western Asia

Minor, and its chief city of Thyatira was filled with trade guilds, the ancient world's equivalent of labor unions. Many of these trade guilds had to do with the manufacture of fabric—clothiers, braziers, and dyers. Thyatira was a center of commerce and industry that provided the perfect place for an industrious and intelligent woman to learn her craft and become positioned for opportunity when it came—the ideal environment to prepare her to become a success story.

Additionally, Thyatira was a melting pot of many nationalities. The cosmopolitan nature of the region has been confirmed by the diversity of names that have been discovered on ancient monuments. This diversity was also reflected in the area's bent toward a polytheistic religious expression. The chief object of devotion was Apollo, worshiped as the sun god under the name Tyrannus, but he was only one of many gods. In light of this environment of religious pluralism, it is perhaps not surprising that the church of Thyatira was the recipient of one of Jesus' seven letters to the churches, which chastened the believers there for allowing a Jezebel to give them spiritual direction, but also commended them for their overarching faithfulness in their service to God (Revelation 2:18–24). This, then, was the culture, industry, and religious atmosphere from which Lydia came.

At some point, however, she left Asia Minor and moved to Philippi, the major city of Macedonia (what is today northern Greece), which was a two-day journey across the Aegean Sea following almost 150 miles of travel to the coast from the Lydian province—not an easy trip in the first century. She may have relocated in Philippi for any number of reasons, but one contributing factor may have been that the people of Philippi had a much broader view of women's rights than the culture in Asia Minor. As a result, women had more freedom in Philippi than in Thyatira, and it was that measure of freedom that allowed her to become a successful businesswoman.

Upon relocating to Philippi, Lydia would have found a very small Jewish community. This is evidenced by the Jewish assembly having to pray by the river, implying that they had no synagogue (Acts 16:13). According to Jewish law, a community needed ten men to form a synagogue, without which no formal worshiping community could be established. Later, partially as a result of Lydia's own influence, Philippi became the site of the first European church and received one of Paul's prison epistles and one of his most beloved letters, Philippians. It also was the hometown of Epaphroditus, a colleague of the apostle Paul who ministered with him, even to the point of death (Philippians 2:25–27).

All of this paints a fascinating picture. Lydia, a successful Asian woman, leaves the restrictiveness of Thyatira to attempt her business advancements in the more open Philippi. Both were pagan towns with pagan gods, yet both became centers of Christian worship in the ancient world. And Lydia was heavily involved in the founding of the church in Philippi.

A Life of Focus

Thousands of women have attended the University of North Carolina—but only one Mia Hamm. Thousands of women have competed in intercollegiate women's soccer—but only one Mia Hamm. Thousands of women have skillfully and passionately represented their nations in international athletic competition—but only one Mia Hamm.

Mia Hamm is a remarkable soccer athlete who grew up in a nation that had about as much interest in soccer as it had in the various species of snails, and only marginally more interest in women's sports. Women's sports, in general, do not generate anywhere near the interest that men's sports do, and that is compounded by the fact that soccer has never really caught on in the United States (a fact I am well aware of as a result of being a goalie on my college's varsity soccer team). Yet, along with her teammates, Hamm's focus, determination, skill, and grace lifted the sport of soccer to a point of near fan frenzy when the US women's soccer team began its march to the 1999 Women's World Cup soccer championship. It was a remarkable victory that was made all the more noteworthy by the maturity and style with which one woman became the face of that victory. That one face was Mia Hamm, a woman focused on a goal that few people cared about until the goal was achieved.

It is not uncommon for a woman to have to be five times better than a man to prove herself or to be recognized as just as capable in a given field. Today, Mia Hamm is just such a woman. In the first century, Lydia was that woman, and she was dealing with more obstacles than the United States women's soccer team ever imagined. But she had the focus and determination to become successful in spite of and in the midst of a world set against her.

Lydia was, according to Acts 16:14, a "seller of purple fabrics." In a single phrase, this tells us a great deal about her. Her hometown of Thyatira was famous for the manufacture of purple cloth, and no doubt that is where she learned her skills and some of the ins and outs of the fabric industry of her day. A critical factor in the development and success of the trade guild of dyers and the craft of dying cloth in the area of Thyatira was largely due to the water, which was uniquely suited to bring out the bright red and rich purple dyes that were in great demand. One reason for this demand was that purple was the color of the official imperial stripe on the togas worn throughout the Roman Empire. From what we are told about her in Acts, we know that Lydia became a successful dealer in purple cloth and also a woman of some wealth.

- Selling the expensive purple cloth was a brisk, competitive market, yet Lydia had become noteworthy in this field. She is identified first as "a seller of purple [cloth] from the city of Thyatira" (v. 14 NKJV).

- She would not have had servants unless she had amassed significant wealth. Acts speaks of "[the members of] her household" (v. 15), which usually refers to servants.

- She had the means to care for Paul and his followers (at least four men), funding their needs and supporting their work. This is implied in her invitation for them to stay in her home.

- To have risen to the top of her field in a world vastly more male-dominated than today's, Lydia must have been a woman of industry, diligence, and hard work—all qualities of the virtuous woman described in Proverbs 31. Yet, much of the description of the Proverbs 31 woman has to do with the honor she brings to her husband. So, what about Lydia—was she married?

The text doesn't tell us, but hints lead us to believe she was not married. In that culture, if she were married her husband most likely would have been the dealer or merchant. Though a woman was expected to work, and work hard, for the family's benefit, it was the husband who was the "face" of the business to the mostly masculine customers they dealt with. In a world where women in general and wives in particular were supposed to remain anonymous, Lydia was a successful member of the business community, so it is unlikely that she was married. (As an interesting note, some Bible scholars speculate that she later married Paul and that she is the "true yokefellow" Paul mentions in Philippians 4:3 KJV.)

As far as we can tell from the evidence, though, Lydia was a single woman, successful in business, hard-working and determined, who made a major move from one country to another to expand her opportunities for success. Amazingly, in Philippi she would find wealth beyond her wildest dreams without ever finding a penny!

A Life of Faith

In Acts 16:14 we read, "Now a certain woman named Lydia heard us. She was a seller of purple from the city of Thyatira, who worshiped God" (NKJV). The phrase "worshiped God" implies that Lydia, if not Jewish, was at the very least a proselyte to Judaism, much like Cornelius (Acts 10). The old rabbinic term used to describe Gentile converts to Judaism was "the God-Fearers." Acts 10 says of Cornelius:

91

- He was devout, reflecting a heart of devotion to God.
- He feared God, revealing a heart of reverence toward God.
- He gave alms to the Jewish people, displaying a heart of compassion for the chosen people of God.
- He prayed to God continually, exhibiting a heart of dependence upon God.

Lydia, too, was a "God-Fearer." If she was not Jewish by birth, she may have become interested in Judaism while living in Thyatira, where there was a large Jewish community. And when she left her home in Asia Minor, she took her adopted faith with her. Now, in Philippi, she had connected with a small group of Jews who had to go miles away to the riverside to pray (v. 13). Still, Lydia was faithful to her convictions and stayed true to Jehovah. She made the effort and the sacrifice to do what was right. Two strong lessons come from this:

- She had a prepared heart. Lydia knew about God, was committed to Him, and was prepared to find a personal relationship with Him.
- She had her priorities straight. Often, business and career people are so deeply involved in their vocational responsibilities that they allow no time for spiritual things. Not Lydia! She faithfully went to pray and to seek God. And as major as her personal and professional victories may have been, this was a matter eternally more important than commercial success.

Her heart, drawn to faith and ready for it, had moved Lydia from her homeland to a strange land, from a position of secondary status to one of leadership and influence, and perhaps even from paganism to Judaism. All of this positioned her for a far greater life transition—one that would occur in a most unlikely place.

A Life Forgiven

Luke, the beloved physician and colleague of the apostle Paul, recorded the life-changing encounter that took place "down by the riverside."

> And a certain woman named Lydia, a seller of purple, of the city of Thyatira, which worshipped God, heard us: whose heart the Lord opened, that she attended unto the things which were spoken of Paul. And when she was baptized, and her household, she besought us, saying, If ye have judged me to be faithful to the Lord, come into my house, and abide there. And she constrained us (Acts 16:14–15 KJV).

Outwardly, this conversion and baptism of one woman and her household would seem to be a meager breakthrough for Paul, especially in the light of what it took to bring this all about.

Earlier, Paul had entered Asia Minor with a desire to preach, but the Holy Spirit had forbidden him to do so (Acts 16:6). The small band of missionaries, including Paul and Silas, had traveled west until they reached the coast of ancient Turkey, and still the Lord did not permit Paul to engage in his preaching ministry. Then, when they reached Troas, God spoke to Paul in a dream. Paul saw a man calling to him, "Come over to Macedonia and help us" (v. 9)—and the world was changed forever. After receiving what has been called "the Macedonian vision," Paul took the gospel west into Europe, instead of going east into Asia, and the socio-political impact of that decision is still felt in our world today!

Paul crossed from Asia (Turkey) into Europe (Greece) and thus came to Philippi, which was the third city on his route after he had responded to the call to minister the message of Christ in Macedonia (vv. 11–12). Here, his first opportunity to share Christ was with a small group of women who were gathered outside the city gates near the river (v. 13).

As Paul faithfully presented the message of Christ to these women, the wonderful paradox of salvation was at work—man's involvement with people and God's work in a heart:

- Paul spoke the Word. We have been given the human responsibility to share the message of the Savior with the entire world.
- The Lord opened Lydia's heart. Only God can do what no preacher or evangelist can do, as His divine intervention works in the hearts of those in need of redemption.
- She responded, obeyed, and was baptized. We have the human responsibility to respond to the offer of salvation with faith.

As evidence of her faith, Lydia was baptized and her servants followed her example! This career woman who had risen above so many challenges to become successful, who had worked so hard to earn her way to the top in a thoroughly male culture, now had experienced grace. Humanly speaking, her life was successful, deeply rooted in the ethics of hard work. Now, however, through the free gift of salvation and the forgiveness of her sins, her life exhibited something far greater. Though her diligence and industriousness had given her a measure of material wealth and security, she had been freely given eternal riches in Christ and a confident hope of eternity. Lydia had the honor of being the first convert on European soil, and the forerunner of all in the West who have come to Christ since.

It is impossible to overstate the significance of this event. In a world where women were viewed as property, this woman was offered the grace of Jesus Christ and believed in Him!

The New Testament records many instances of women who came to Christ and found hope. Women who were considered "down and out," women of suspect character and questionable morals, who found forgiveness. Women of skepticism and doubt who found reason to believe. Here, however, we find something far different. We see a woman of prayer, a woman successful and reputable in the eyes of the watching world, find real life. Lydia's declaration of faith in Jesus Christ is a vivid reminder that the Lord of heaven came to redeem all, not just some. She is the poster child for the reality that the gospel is a message of everlasting life to everyone, whether they seem to have it made in this life or not.

A famous and outspoken television executive once remarked that Christianity is "a religion for losers." Lydia proves it is not. No matter how successful we are, we do not really experience success until we come to Christ.

Salvation is needed by all and is offered freely: "whoso-ever will, let him take the water of life freely" (Revelation 22:17 KJV).

A Life of Faithfulness

I have had the privilege of teaching and serving with the Moscow Theological Institute. As a result, I have been blessed with warm friendships in a hard land that shows no pity for people who have little or nothing. It is a nation largely without hope, bent on day-to-day, hand-to-mouth survival. In the midst of that harsh world, Tamara Platova radiates the grace of Christ. She is my "Moscow mom," and she lives out the heart of a servant, not out of duty or subjugation but out of love—love for Christ and love for His people. I have seen Tamara, now in her sixties, work eighty hours a week serving the staff, students, and visiting teachers of the institute—and never does her smile fade, never does her joy dissipate, never does the tedious work seem unimportant to her. Daily, she manifests the truth in her heart in countless ways, not the least of which is her kindness to others.

Lydia, the successful career woman, practiced her faith the same way, exhibiting the heart of a servant and a will-ingness to care for the needs of others, beginning with those she knew best. After her expression of personal faith, she first reached out to her own servants and then offered her resources in service of the gospel. "When she and the mem-bers of her household were baptized, she invited us to her home. 'If you consider me a believer in the Lord,' she said, 'come and stay at my house.' And she persuaded us" (Acts 16:15 NIV).

Gratitude to Christ prompted Lydia to do something for His cause. She prevailed upon Paul and his company to stay in her home and let her serve them and minister to them. In doing this, she demonstrated something the Bible commends to us frequently: the grace of hospitality.

- Let love of the brethren continue. Do not neglect to show hospitality to strangers, for by this some have entertained angels without knowing it (Hebrews 13:1–2).
- Be kind to one another, tender-hearted, forgiving each other, just as God in Christ also has forgiven you (Ephesians 4:32).
- Contributing to the needs of the saints, practicing hospitality (Romans 12:13).
- "The King will answer and say to them, 'Truly I say to you, to the extent that you did it to one of these brothers of Mine, even the least of them, you did it to Me'" (Matthew 25:40).

As done unto Him! In these simple deeds of hospitality are the fingerprints of Christ Himself. Those fingerprints were all over Lydia's life and the lives she touched in His name, for her commitment to faithful service would not end with a token gesture of kindness. In Acts 16:40 we read: "And they went out of the prison and entered the house of Lydia, and when they saw the brethren, they encouraged them and departed."

Lydia opened her home to the church, and thus her home became a center for Christian influence in the city of Philippi. When her heart was opened to the Savior, her home was opened to her new family—the community of faith.

Though mentioned only briefly in the New Testament, Lydia is a fascinating portrait of the power of the cross to change a life. But she is also a wonderful reminder of what a believing heart does to express the love it has received. She was a woman of strength in a world that was threatened by such strength, yet she acknowledged her own spiritual weakness and found true strength in Christ. Lydia is an example of a woman of faith that can be embraced by the most successful women in our day.

In my work at RBC Ministries I am continually amazed at the remarkable and talented people who make up our staff. Among these are some of the most savvy and skilled women I have ever known. Our human resources director, Janine, is one of those women. A colleague who recently joined the staff and has just been through the hiring and orientation process says this about Janine's skill and professionalism: "She is sharp. She could direct any corporation in this town!" But Janine has committed her talents, gifts, and insight to advancing the cause of the Savior through the efforts of this ministry.

Obviously this doesn't mean that Christian women can find fulfillment only in a Christian organization, but when I see Janine and women like her whose lives are committed to the Lord and His work, I think of Lydia. I look back over twenty-five years of pastoral ministry and am reminded of Betsy, Patty, Carol, and other godly women who were crucial to the work of the church. I am also reminded that, in most churches, it is godly women who do most of the heavy lifting of the work of ministry—and I thank God for their heart of service, as well as their skill and grace.

Godly, talented, successful women of faith serving Christ and impacting eternity are a true gift from God. May the tribe of Lydia increase, for, humanly, the church cannot get by without them.

Principles from the Life of Lydia

Several significant attitudes come into the spotlight when we consider the life of Lydia:

- ◆ Attitude #1. Worship takes precedence over work. Though successful in business, Lydia was in the place of worship when her community of faith met to worship.

- ◆ Attitude #2. Hospitality and sharing are a life priority when you have been a recipient of grace. Having received the free gift of salvation, Lydia freely offered whatever she had to others in need. Personal greed and selfishness have no place in a redeemed heart.

- ◆ Attitude #3. Allow the Word of God to challenge our hearts, especially when we think we have life under control! No wealth or power or success could have compared to what Lydia received when she opened her heart to the message of the cross.

6
Martha

A Misunderstood Life

A popular soft drink used to be advertised as the "most misunderstood soft drink in the world." Apparently the buying public didn't understand that concept of misunderstanding to be a good thing, so the company's marketers had to return to the drawing board. In the following years, they experimented with a variety of different slogans before landing on "Taste the Original"—and sales increased.

Misunderstanding can be costly. It can also have enormous repercussions.

In the years following the First World War, Germany was a broken nation. Humbled and humiliated, the German people lived under the specter of international scrutiny and restrictions. Forbidden by the Versailles Treaty to develop any kind of military presence, and struggling under a horribly depressed economy, Germany was a mere shadow of its former greatness under the kaiser. Then, a short, mustachioed, charismatic corporal from Bavaria began preaching a nationalistic message of hope and optimism, something for which the people were desperate. But few understood the man's true mission. Few had read his rambling, lengthy (hundreds of pages) philosophy, *Mein Kampf,* which foreshadowed the Holocaust with his passion for an ethnically cleansed Europe and gave the blueprint for the Third Reich. Only his inner circle realized the scope of his maniacal strategy—a strategy that would plunge the world into a second global conflict.

What the people saw and heard instead was someone who had vision and passion, and they embraced him. Would they have done so had they truly understood him? For most people, probably not. But Adolf Hitler rose to power on the backs of people who understood too little and believed too much. Imagine how different the world might be today if people had only understood clearly what the new chancellor of Germany was plotting. Paul Harvey would have called that "the rest of the story."

Misunderstanding can be a very dangerous thing. And not just in world events. Biblical misunderstanding can be threatening to us and to the very life of the church.

The Christian community is often guilty of misunderstanding or misapplying the truth of the Scriptures by working off assumption rather than careful study, usually because we don't make an effort to understand. We find enough information on the surface to draw some conclusions, and we never push behind those surface elements to grasp the full depth of biblical truth, settling for the letter rather than the spirit of the law. Admittedly this seldom invokes a world war (although it sometimes feels like it in the life of a church!), but this kind of misunderstanding can lead us to serious misjudgments, which in turn can cause division, hurt feelings, and even wasted resources. As

101

Haddon Robinson has said, God has given us a compass more than a roadmap in the Bible, and it requires careful reading.

One area where this kind of misunderstanding is especially noticeable is in our view of certain Bible characters. And one character who has been the victim of just such misunderstanding is Martha. In our preaching and teaching she is almost always characterized in the same negative way. But I believe she has gotten a bad rap because her story is usually only partially told, leaving her misunderstood and also misjudged. So let's look at the rest of the story.

◆

Martha is such a familiar biblical character that it's easy to assume that we already know her very well. We have heard her story, seen her failure, and labeled her accordingly. But what if we've missed something? Let's take a second look and ask the question, "What do we really know about Martha?"

As is the case with many of our biblical character studies, we start with that which we most take for granted: her name. Martha is the feminine form of *moro*, which means "lord" or "master." It is a word that speaks of authority, so much so that the masculine form of *moro* is *maran*, found in maran-atha—the *Lord* comes. There is no biblical evidence that this was a nickname; it appears instead to have been her given name, and one she seems to live up to when she seeks to take charge of a situation and "run it."

Martha's family is also familiar to us: her sister Mary and her brother Lazarus. The three—we are not told of any other family members—lived together in the little village of Bethany just east of Jerusalem on the far side of the Mount of Olives.

Because Martha lived with her brother and sister, it is reasonable to assume that she was unmarried (as was Mary). The Bible seems to indicate that they were a family of means and that they used that means in support of the ministry of the Master, Christ Himself. In fact, John 11:5 says that the relationship between Jesus and this family was a special one indeed: "Jesus loved Martha and her sister and Lazarus." Because of the way Martha has been painted over the years, we might have reversed that order! Lazarus, whose death caused the Savior to weep, should come first; Mary the loving worshiper should at least be second; and Martha, whose priorities were askew, should come last—right? Yet, John, writing years later and with the benefit of hindsight, places Martha first in the list, and I find that not only compelling but a strong hint of the level of our misunderstanding of Martha.

Much of that misunderstanding, I suspect, comes from the fact that Martha is seldom, if ever, considered apart from her sister, who, as we will see, has favored status in our thinking. This tendency to lump the two sisters together was noted by Herbert Lockyer in his wonderful volume *All the Women of the Bible.*

Martha and Mary seem to belong together in God's portrait gallery, just as Cain and Abel and Jacob and Esau do. Expositors also bracket the two sisters together, comparing and contrasting their respective traits. Martha, busy with household chores—Mary, preferring to sit before Jesus for spiritual instruction. Martha, ever active and impulsive—Mary, meditative and reticent. Truly drawn are the characters of these two sisters, Martha usually busy supervising the hospitality of the home, Mary, somewhat indifferent to housework, anxious only to seek that which was spiritual. But we have no scriptural warrant for affirming that the

difference between quiet, pious Mary and her industrious
sister is that of the opposite of light to darkness. In the
church there are vessels of gold and others of silver, but
we are not justified in saying that the character of Mary is
worked in gold and that of Martha in silver. These two sisters in that Bethany family had their respective, appropriate talents, and each of them served the Master accordingly
(Lockyer, *All the Women of the Bible*, 87).

I agree with Dr. Lockyer. Thus, I would ask that, as we
bring Martha into the spotlight on center stage, we agree
to level the playing field a bit. Both Mary and Martha were
sinful, flawed human beings. Both were also wonderful
women. And both had lessons to learn from the Christ.
Considering these things, then, let's push past our misunderstanding of Martha and look for some valuable insights
on Christian living.

A Distracted Heart

I have to confess that when I am preaching I am absolutely distracted. I get so intensely focused on what I am
doing that almost anything could happen and I would be
totally oblivious. When I was a pastor, it was not unusual
for my wife, as we drove home from church, to ask me if I
had noticed what had happened somewhere in the sanctuary during the service; invariably I would be clueless, having no idea what she was talking about. You could set off
a bomb under the pulpit and, unless physically incapable
of doing so, I would probably just keep right on preaching.

This kind of focus can be good, but it can also be a problem. At one point in my pastoral ministry I noticed that the
wife of one of our deacons seemed to be unhappy with me,

and I couldn't figure out what I had done to upset her. Finally I gave up trying to figure it out and just asked her if she was upset with me. Her hesitant response was that yes, in fact, she was very unhappy with me. When I asked her why, she said that several weeks before, I had walked past her without speaking when I was on my way into the auditorium for the worship service. I had no idea that I had done this. I asked her forgiveness, and she gladly granted the pardon. It was not my intention to be rude or aloof; I was just so focused on preparing my heart and mind to preach and the preaching itself that I missed most of what was going on around me in the morning service time.

I wonder if Martha suffered from the same problem. When we first come upon her, she is so zoned in on her activity that she misses some things that matter an awful lot. "Now it happened as they went that [Jesus] entered a certain village; and a certain woman named Martha welcomed Him into her house. And she had a sister called Mary, who also sat at Jesus' feet and heard His word" (Luke 10:38–39 NKJV).

Martha carried the responsibility for hospitality in their home, and it is a responsibility that she took very seriously. Some have speculated that this was because Martha was the eldest, and such speculation has merit. Her actions as well as her bearing seem to picture someone accustomed to having to take charge, especially in matters of the household. In that culture, as in many cultures around the world today, the woman of the house was judged, sometimes harshly, by her skill or lack of it in caring for guests in her home. So Martha was committed to making certain that Christ and His men received good treatment and a proper welcome.

Mary, however, did not share her priorities. While Martha was busy preparing food and providing comfort for their guests, Mary simply sat at Jesus' feet, listening to His teaching.

In the midst of her busyness, Martha's frustration boiled to the surface. Being polite about her feelings was not as important to her as pointing out the fact that Mary was not doing her part! "But Martha was distracted with all her preparations; and she came up to Him and said, 'Lord, do You not care that my sister has left me to do all the serving alone? Then tell her to help me.'"

We could wonder why Martha went to Jesus and not to Mary herself. Perhaps it was because she had tired of confronting her sister on a chronic matter. Perhaps it was to make sure that the Master knew how hard she was working. Perhaps it was to add some much-needed clout to her appeal. Of one thing I am convinced, however. I don't think Martha intended anyone to see her frustration or hear her demand of the Master except Christ Himself. Still, someone else did hear, and Luke recorded the incident for the entire world to read about for centuries to come!

Something similar happened following the death of my grandfather. After the funeral, the family gathered at the old homestead in Roanoke, Virginia, for a meal together before we all headed back to our own homes. I come from a large family, so the house was packed—filled with people, noise, and not a little chaos. One of my sisters tried to organize everyone by giving orders and instructions about what was to happen next and why. But the more she tried to get everyone in line, the more chaotic it became, ratcheting up her frustration level and her intensity with it! Then, one of my brothers-in-law became frustrated with her frustration. As she shouted instructions, he finally had his fill. It was one of those quirky times when, in the midst of a noisy room, it suddenly got quiet—just at the instant my brother-in-law shouted, "Who died and left you in charge?" He intended that only my sister hear him, but everyone did!

His indignation was apparent to everyone in the room, as was Martha's when she complained to Christ. Jesus' response, however, was the very image of patience—especially in the face of her impatience. "But the Lord answered and said to her, 'Martha, Martha, you are worried and bothered about so many things; but only one is necessary, for Mary has chosen the good part, which shall not be taken away from her'" (Luke 10:41–42).

In no way did Jesus imply that what Martha was doing was irrelevant or insignificant. It simply did not have the eternal value that Mary's choice displayed. Mary chose worship, and that "one thing" is to take priority over human-directed activity. When Jesus used the phrase "one thing," He reminded Martha of the need for lasting values, challenging her to keep things in proper perspective and using the same Greek expression that is used frequently in the New Testament to point to priorities:

- Mark 10:21: Christ challenged the "rich young ruler" who had come professing faith. In the midst of a profound declaration of spiritual commitment, Jesus focused on the young man's heart like a laser by saying, "*One thing* you lack: go and sell all you possess and . . . follow Me" (emphasis added).

THE SPOTLIGHT OF FAITH

- John 9:25: When Christ healed the man born blind, the religious establishment questioned the legitimacy of the event. When pressed for an explanation, the formerly blind man could only respond, "*One thing* I know: that though I was blind, now I see" (NKJV, emphasis added).
- Philippians 3:13–14: When the apostle Paul was explaining his spiritual journey to his readers, he told them how he had moved beyond religious pedigree and performance to a relationship with Christ that he pursued with all his heart. His desire? "*One thing* I do: forgetting what lies behind and reaching forward to what lies ahead, I press on toward the goal for the prize of the upward call of God in Christ Jesus" (emphasis added).

Martha needed to embrace the spiritual nourishment that came from the teaching of the Savior.

The disciples had learned after Jesus' encounter with the woman at the well (John 4) that His nourishment came from serving the Father. What was the source of Martha's nourishment? What is ours? Are we focusing on the "one thing," or are we distracted by the "many things" of life?

A Declared Faith

The next time we see Martha, she and her family are facing tragedy head-on (John 11). As the story begins, we learn that Lazarus, the brother of Mary and Martha, is ill. The sisters send a message to Jesus, telling Him that "he whom You love is sick." Without fully explaining His reasons to the disciples, Jesus does not respond immediately. When He does finally lead the disciples to Bethany (in the shadows of the danger that is brewing in Jerusalem), He announces to them that, in fact, Lazarus is already dead. And by the time they arrive at Bethany, Lazarus has been entombed for four days. The mourners are still there offering a sad mixture of grief and comfort when they arrive, and Martha comes out to meet Jesus. "Martha therefore, when she heard that Jesus was coming, went to meet Him, but Mary stayed at the house. Martha then said to Jesus, 'Lord, if You had been here, my brother would not have died'" (John 11:20–21).

Martha's words seem to have a bite to them, as if she were saying, "How could You let us down like this?" But that is not the case, as evidenced in her next comment: "Even now I know that whatever You ask of God, God will give You" (John 11:22).

Even in the midst of her grief, Martha declares her confidence in Christ's ability and in His relationship with the Father. She had believed it before Lazarus' death, and she continues to believe it in spite of Lazarus' death.

When Jesus then probes her faith further, she affirms the belief that was commonly held by first-century Jews: that Lazarus would rise in the resurrection to come (v. 24). Jesus, however, does not let up. And His next declaration to her remains one of the great theological statements in the New Testament: "I am the resurrection and the life; he who believes in Me will live even if he dies, and everyone who lives and believes in Me will never die. Do you believe this?" (John 11:25–26).

It is here that we begin to catch a glimpse of Martha's true heart! Her declaration of faith is full and comprehensive, heartfelt and sound. She has embraced the teaching and heart of the Master, and now, even in the midst of her

109

pain and grief, that trust rings forth with boldness and vigor: "Yes, Lord; I have believed that You are the Christ, the Son of God, even He who comes into the world" (John 11:27).

Notice the completeness of her answer. She declares that Jesus is nothing less than . . .

The Christ.

The Son of God.

The One who comes into the world.

Big words! Big ideas. Bold statements. In fact, Martha's affirmation is reminiscent of Peter's declaration of faith at Caesarea Philippi, which prompted Jesus to attribute the statement to the Father's guidance (Matthew 16).

In Martha's interaction with Jesus He had stretched her faith, and in every instance she had responded to the challenge with utter confidence in Him. In fact, Martha's words to Jesus take her relationship with Him to another level—a level to which Mary doesn't go when given the same opportunity (John 11:32). In the midst of the identical experience of loss, Martha's words are filled with hope and confidence. Mary, however, is so ruled by her grief that all she can feel is disappointment that the Master has not come in time. Like Martha, she says, "Lord, if you had been here, my brother would not have died." Unfortunately, Mary stops there. She does not declare confidence in Christ's relationship with His Father, or in the power of Jesus to reverse this tragic event, as has Martha. With Mary, no expression of hope follows— just the pain of emptiness and loss. How different are the responses of these two sisters to the death of their brother!

How or why was this maturing of Martha's relationship with Jesus possible? I would suggest, and there is good reason to believe this, that Martha was not always in the kitchen, and that she took Jesus' gentle rebuke in Luke 10 and acted on it. Martha, too, spent time at Jesus' feet, where she heard and understood His teaching and appropriated it into her life. The result? In the darkest moment of her life—at least in the portion of her life that we know about—she turned to Jesus by faith and entrusted Him with her heart and with the well-being of those she loved most.

Granted, Martha still doesn't completely understand the power of Christ to fully reverse the laws of nature and bring undiminished life out of death. This is evidenced by her questioning the wisdom of opening Lazarus' tomb when Jesus tells them to remove the stone. "Lord, by this time there will be a stench; for he has been dead four days," she responds, her strong, practical side coming out once again. But her faith is no less remarkable because of those words. Interestingly, in this situation, Mary does not express the same confidence in Christ that Martha displays, giving us plenty of grounds to reconsider the negative evaluation that is usually made of Martha's spiritual heart.

The lesson here is so very practical—and so vital. Much of what we become as people is dependent upon how we react to correction. Martha was challenged by Jesus and could have responded any number of ways. She could have become angry, bitter, embarrassed, or reactionary. She chose instead to be instructed, and it gave her the opportunity to grow, which positioned her for great faith when she needed it the most, at the death of her brother.

A Dedicated Life

At some point in our own spiritual journeys, the thing that really matters is commitment—a determined dedication to being followers of Christ. This powerful spiritual principle was captured clearly in the Academy Award winning film *Chariots of Fire,* which presents the true story of missionary/track star Eric Liddell, who was asked to set aside his values and principles for a temporal prize in the 1924 Paris Olympics. His singular devotion to be true to his spiritual convictions fueled the wrath of some of his countrymen who questioned his loyalty to king and country, drew the admiration of his opponents who saw him as a man of true character, and caused puzzlement among those people who saw values as something that could quickly be jettisoned if they did not suit the mood of the mob or the pressures of the moment. Liddell believed it was wrong to run on Sundays, and he was willing to lose the opportunity to represent his country in the Olympics rather than compromise those convictions, which he believed were an echo of the voice of the Scriptures in his heart. Liddell was a man of character and commitment in a world of compromise. And because he resisted the pressures of the world, he became a model of devotion and dedication, choosing the way of the cross over the way of the crowd.

Dedication means that we are committed to doing what is right, even when it is not easy, not popular, or not noticed. It means we do what's right because it is right—not because we think there is a prize ahead. Dedication also brings a heart of service the satisfaction it longs for, but not at the expense of principles. It makes spiritual service an act of worship instead of mere empty activity.

We see this kind of devotion in Martha: her correction by the Savior led to faith that, in turn, led to dedication. In a passage easily overlooked, we see the end result of her journey toward trust in Christ.

Then, six days before the Passover, Jesus came to Bethany, where Lazarus was who had been dead, whom He had raised from the dead. There they made Him a supper; and Martha served, but Lazarus was one of those who sat at the table with Him. Then Mary took a pound of very costly oil of spikenard, anointed the feet of Jesus, and wiped His feet with her hair. And the house was filled with the fragrance of the oil (John 12:1–3 NKJV).

In a subtle way, John pictures the lessons that Martha has learned throughout her experience with the Master. As we compare the scene to the Luke 10 passage, we see some strong similarities—and one major difference. The similarities are clear:

- Once again the scene is the home of Lazarus in Bethany. The text of John 11–12 makes it clear that Lazarus had not only reached the status of first-century rock star; he, like Jesus, had also become a threat to the religious establishment. They wanted to kill him for being raised from the dead (John 12:10). In an amazing display of unbelief, they wanted to kill Jesus for raising Lazarus from the dead, and kill Lazarus for being raised! But here in his home, Lazarus sits safely at the table with Jesus—a living man and his life-giving Savior!
- Once again it is suppertime. The man Jesus had raised from the dead is now hosting "a dinner . . . given in Jesus' honor" (NIV). It is this family's attempt to say "thank you" for their brother's life, and an attempt to recognize the Christ for who He is.
- Once again Mary is at Jesus' feet. And she expresses her worship the only way she knows how. She takes a flask of valuable perfume and anoints Jesus' feet, then shows

113

her utter submission to Christ by wiping His feet with her hair. Paul wrote that the glory of a woman is her hair (1 Corinthians 11). Mary submits her glory to Christ's in preparation for His death and burial (John 12:7).

But what about Martha? Well, once again, she is serving—but this time is different (v. 2). This time, Martha's service is offered without complaint. She has learned from her failure in the past, and from her faith for the future. She has learned to serve Jesus from the heart. She has learned the joy of devotion.

Martha had learned that greatest of all spiritual lessons: contentment in Christ. Mary expressed her worship through perfume and adoration. Martha presented her worship through cooking and serving. Mary's act of worship was noticed by all. Martha's act of worship was less noticeable, but no less profound. Like Joseph in Potiphar's house and Egypt's prisons (Genesis 37–41), she was content to serve where she was. No fanfare, no front-row seat, no public acknowledgment was necessary. She had learned how to be happy in doing her behind-the-scenes work, and doing it for the Lord. Contentment with her role and her ministry had made a life-changing difference in Martha's heart.

◆

When I was in Bible college, one of our chapel speakers once made this strong and uncompromising statement: "Some of you here are studying to be pastors. I want you to know that you are unusually blessed, for there is no calling in life that is as high as the calling to the pastorate."

I was one of those students studying for pastoral ministry, but I was troubled by his words. It seemed to me (and it still does) that the highest calling we can have is the one to which God calls us, whether it is as a construction worker, a homemaker, an educator, a person in full-time ministry, or a plethora of other occupations. No matter what we do in life, there is no greater calling than being faithful to the task God has given us.

Also, I once heard a pastor say that in the church today we have too many Marthas and not enough Marys. I couldn't disagree more. Martha's dedication was not less than Mary's. Her service was just as pleasing to Christ as her sister's. She just needed to embrace that calling and live it out with faith and joy. What we truly need today is an army of Christ-followers with Mary's heart of worship and Martha's hands of service—all dedicated to our living Lord.

"Whatever your hand finds to do, do it with all your might" (Ecclesiastes 9:10).

Principles from the Life of Martha

- Though activity and busyness have their proper place in our lives, worship must be given priority.

- Faith must be allowed victory over our heartbreaking life situations.

- Learning from correction is a critical step forward in our progress toward spiritual maturity.

- Why we do what we do is as important as what we do—perhaps even more important.

7

Miriam

THE SISTER

"It's like kissing your sister!" Ever heard that expression? In sports vernacular, this intentionally distasteful phrase is used to describe a game that ends in a tie score. Now, I understand the intended meaning pretty well because I have three sisters. The one with whom I am closest is my sister Carole, who is six years my junior, and although we now have a great relationship, we had anything but that when we were growing up. In fact, we didn't get along at all—mostly because she was a whiny little girl who always had to have her own way (I hasten to add that, to my knowledge, I contributed nothing to our inability to get along). So the thought of kissing my sister . . . yuck!

By the time we were adults, but still practicing the fine art of sibling rivalry, the two of us were asked to sing the national anthem at a minor league baseball game near our hometown, in Charleston, West Virginia. It was a corporate sponsorship night, which meant an unusually large crowd—four to five thousand people. As we walked onto the field, I told Carole to look at the flag not the crowd, to sing the song as fast as we could without dishonoring it, and to help me remember the way to the gate so that we could get off the field as quickly as possible. The announcer introduced the anthem over the public-address system, the organist gave us the first chord, and we were on our way. (I even have a picture to commemorate the evening.) But the crowd was there to watch a ballgame, not to hear two amateurs sing "The Star Spangled Banner," so the last notes of the song were drowned out by the cries "Play ball!" from the stands, and Carole and I made a beeline for the gate and quickly blended into the comfortable anonymity of the bleachers.

I am happy to report that we lived through that night, and even happier to report that we were not invited for a return engagement. But I learned a great lesson that day: few things bond people together quite as well as shared terror. As Samuel Johnson said, "Depend upon it, sir, when a man knows he is to be hanged in a fortnight, it concentrates his mind wonderfully." Exactly right. We focused on the task at hand, got all the words right, and Carole hit the high note at the end. People in the crowd told us it was great, but we never would have known. Our minds were on one thing. Our shared experience melted away our differences and united us in pursuit of one common goal—survival. Believe me, in that moment of terror, kissing my sister was far preferable to facing the crowd at Watt Powell Park in Charleston that summer evening. It was a moment that gave us a rather unique bond, and moved us past many of the rocky, difficult growing-up-in-a-home-of-seven-kids days.

As I think back over the years—with all their ups and downs—I have many fond memories of wonderful experiences with my sisters, as well as some not-so-pleasant, never-to-be-repeated ones, as we have shared life's journey to this point. And it is because of those relationships that I find it so interesting that one of the leading characters in the Bible (maybe the leading character in the Old Testament) had a sister with whom he shared life's journey as well. His name was Moses, and her name was Miriam.

A Godly Woman's Beginnings

In Bible times, children were often named on the basis of the life experiences of their parents, on the parents' expectations for the child, or on the child's character. When Isaac's son Jacob was born, he was named "usurper" because even in birth he grabbed his twin brother's heel, trying to steal the place of his older (if only by moments) brother Esau. Jacob would "live down" to that name by stealing both the paternal blessing and the firstborn's birthright from his older twin.

When Christ was born, He was called Jesus (or Joshua), meaning "Jehovah is Savior," for He was expected to "save His people from their sins" (Matthew 1:21). That expectation became the hope of the world when Jesus went to the cross as the Lamb of God, who, in His own act of self-sacrifice, took away the sins of the world.

From her birth, Moses' sister Miriam was also marked by her name—a strong name, and a name that offered hope, but also carried with it concerns (Exodus 15:20). Herbert Lockyer said that her name is the Hebrew equivalent of the name Mary, or "marah," meaning bitterness, trouble, or rebellion (Lockyer, *All the Women of the Bible*, 111). One form of the word *marah* translates into our word "myrrh," referring to the bitter ointments used in ancient times in the burial process. Another form becomes the New Testament word "Smyrna," which was the New Testament church that suffered the bitterness of persecution (Revelation 2:8–11). Her name could mark her as one who would experience all the hardships of life, or as one who would actually cause some of those hardships. Only time would tell how she would live up to her name.

Miriam was the oldest child of Amram and Jochebed and was the older sister of both Aaron and Moses (Exodus 6:20). She benefited not only from her parent's faith and spiritual confidence, but also from their strong commitment to family. That commitment was evidenced in the rescue of the infant Moses, as all of them risked their lives to rescue a helpless innocent. Jochebed was a model of courage and faith to her daughter—a priceless gift. Without question, Miriam had a life filled with opportunity to observe character and strength!

Despite her prominent place in the history of Israel, however, it is quite fascinating how little we really know about Miriam. Although she was the famous sister of the Old Testament's most famous leader, we are not certain of something as basic as her marital status! In his *Jewish Antiquities*, Flavius Josephus, the first-century Jewish historian, maintains that Miriam became the wife of Hur, one of Israel's judges at Sinai (Exodus 24:14). If so, she would have been the grandmother of Bezaleel who was the craftsman most intimately involved in the building of the tabernacle (Exodus 1:2). Herbert Lockyer, a lifelong student of biblical characters, points out, however, that this is probably not true, and I believe that Lockyer is correct (Lock-yer, *All the Women of the Bible,* 111). Miriam is always referred to as the sister of Moses or the sister of Aaron, which would be an insult to her husband if she were married, particularly since women were frequently referred to as "the wife of . . . ." Extrapolating from the biblical record, then, it is safe to assume that Miriam remained single all her life. And if that is the case, she is a terrific model of how God can use adult singles to accomplish His work in the world. The apostle Paul, who also never married, described the value of singleness with exceptional clarity when he wrote, "But I want you to be free from concern. One who is unmarried is concerned about the things of the Lord, how he may please the Lord" (1 Corinthians 7:32). Miriam concerned herself with the service of Jehovah, and that service began at an early age.

Miriam is usually considered a "minor character" in the Bible. But she is not one of those minor characters who shows up once and then never appears on the scene again. She plays a recurring, supporting role, and each scene in which she appears reveals the continued work of God in molding her life. Sometimes God worked through her submission to Him, while at other times He worked through her failings. But in every instance, the God of Abraham, Isaac, and Jacob was actively involved in the life of this woman.

TAKING A RISK FOR LIFE AND FREEDOM

One of the most horrific examples of man's inhumanity to man is the practice of slavery: turning human beings into property or chattel for monetary gain. Throughout history, many noble men and women have sounded the cry for freedom and stepped forward to fight against slavery, usually because of a fundamental commitment to the God-given value of every human being. William Wilberforce fought for years to bring about political reforms in England that would abolish slavery from the British Empire. Abraham Lincoln played a similar role as the "Great Emancipator" in America. From the conductors on the "underground railroad" that in the mid-1800s stretched from the southern United States to the northern states and Canada, to the efforts of Corrie ten Boom's family to deliver European Jews from the tyranny and torture, slavery and death that awaited them in Hitler's death camps, to a solitary student staring down a tank in China's Tienenmen Square, many of mankind's most courageous moments have come in defense of an individual life's right to be free.

It is in one of those moments that we meet Miriam for the first time, and here we see her at her very best: as a courageous, obedient, and clever young girl.

It was a time of barbaric cruelty. Four hundred years earlier, Joseph, a Hebrew sold into Egyptian slavery by his own brothers, had been God's instrument to bring deliverance and rescue not only to the people of Egypt, but also to the brothers who had betrayed him. In a magnificent act of mercy and forgiveness, Joseph brought his family to Egypt to live in the prosperity of the greatest culture of that day. There the Hebrew children flourished in the shadow of Joseph's protection—and later, his memory—for hundreds of years, until a new king came on the scene in Egypt, a king "who did not know Joseph" (Exodus1:8). This Pharaoh viewed the Hebrews as a threat and enslaved them for his massive construction projects. So intense was his concern about the strength of this slave nation, that he ordered the extermination of all newborn male Hebrew children. He told the Hebrew midwives: "When you are helping the Hebrew women to give birth . . . if it is a son, then you shall put him to death." But the midwives and mothers risked their own lives to give life to the newborn baby boys. They told the king that the Hebrew women were "vigorous"— that they gave birth before a midwife could arrive to assist in the delivery. They feared God more than they feared the threats of Pharaoh (Exodus 1:17), and the result was that the Hebrew people became, in the eyes of the king, an increasingly greater threat to his power. Pharaoh's response was to issue this command: "Every son who is born you are to cast into the Nile" (Exodus 1:15–18, 22).

During this terrible time, Jochebed, Miriam's mother, gave birth to a baby boy—another illegal male Hebrew— and hid the baby for three months (Exodus 2:2). But Jochebed knew she needed a more permanent solution if she were going to save her child. Her solution was to build a wicker basket and cover it with tar and pitch. She then laid her baby boy in this little ark and placed it among the reed beds along the banks of the Nile River. We aren't told what she hoped to accomplish, but it seems clear that she thought the baby's chances for survival were greater in the basket than trying to raise him under the watchful eyes of the slave-masters. (See chapter 4 for more about Jochebed.)

Miriam watched her mother prepare the wicker basket that she hoped would carry her beautiful little brother away from the anger and danger of the pharaoh's paranoia. She continued to watch as her baby brother was placed into the basket, and she watched as the basket—baby Moses' own personal ark—was placed on the waters of the Nile. Then Miriam followed the basket as it floated away, continuing to watch "at a distance" (Exodus 2:4).

How the girl's heart must have pounded when she saw a group of women from the royal household walking down to the water to bathe. Then the most royal among them, the daughter of Pharaoh, spotted the basket among the reeds. She ordered one of her maids to bring it to her, and when she opened the basket, Miriam could hear her brother crying. What was going to happen now?

Pharaoh's daughter was no fool. She immediately realized why this baby had been hidden here. "This is one of the Hebrews' children," she said.

When Miriam saw the look of compassion on the Egyptian woman's face, she did not hesitate. She stepped out of her hiding place and dared to speak to the princess of Egypt! A slave girl offering counsel to royalty was a daring, life-risking act, yet Miriam's courage drove her to brave the moment with advice that the daughter of Pharaoh accepted: "Shall I go and call a nurse for you from the Hebrew women that she may nurse the child for you?" (Exodus 2:7). As a result, Jochebed was able to nurse her own child and care for him during those early years of his life. Some speculate that Moses may have been in his parents' home until he was as much as twelve years old!

Miriam's courageous action meant that her family could still enjoy her baby brother even as they enjoyed the protection and care of the royal family.

It's easy to look at this event through the wrong end of the telescope and assume that Miriam acted in this way because she knew that the baby she protected would be Moses, the deliverer of her people. But nothing in Scripture supports that assumption. I am convinced that she—and her mother—did what she did out of love for family and love for life; that she unknowingly delivered the child who would eventually become *her* deliverer. In an environment of slavery and suffering, when men and women must have seen self-preservation as the prime objective, Miriam risked her life to save the life of her infant brother.

A SONG OF CELEBRATION

We now fast-forward the story eighty or so years to another moment of deliverance. Moses was now a servant of the Hebrew God and had been commissioned by Jehovah to lead the children of Israel out of slavery and into the Land of Promise. Following the Lord's judgment upon Egypt through a series of ten devastating plagues, Pharaoh finally relented and released the Hebrews from their years of slavery. Moses then led the great throng of over two million people to the shores of the Red Sea where they once again faced great danger.

Human memory can be very short. And once the plagues were lifted, Pharaoh began to reconsider. "What is this we have done," he said, "that we have let Israel go from serving us?" (Exodus 14:5). The reality of life without Hebrew slaves was pretty unappealing to the Egyptians, as the slaves were given all the brute tasks that the people of Egypt wanted no part of. Returning those slaves to the quarries and the fields was strategic for the Egyptian economy and lifestyle. When faced with this realization, Pharaoh immediately sent his cavalry to force the Hebrews to return.

Trapped on one side by the waters of the Red Sea and on the other by the Egyptian army, Moses declared, "Do not be afraid. Stand firm and you will see the deliverance the LORD will bring you today. The Egyptians you see today you will never see again. The LORD will fight for you; you need only to be still" (Exodus 14:13–14 NIV).

God did fight for them. He rescued them from the Egyptian chariots by splitting the waters of the sea and giving the Israelites safe passage to the other side, then bringing those same waters crashing down upon Pharaoh's mighty horses and chariots. It was one of the greatest deliverances the world would ever see—over two million slaves carried to safety and freedom by the power of the God of heaven!

By this time, Miriam was ninety to ninety-five years old and must have experienced a myriad of emotions as she watched the baby she had helped rescue decades before become God's instrument of her own rescue and the rescue of an entire nation of people. This penultimate moment was a clear expression of the greatness of God, and only one response would do. As Moses composed an anthem of praise for God's deliverance, Miriam prepared to lead the women of Israel in her own song of praise.

I really love this passage of Scripture. I love it because I love music, and Moses' and Miriam's response to God's powerful deliverance was a musical response. It could be said that worship is primarily acknowledging the perfections of God's character. The word *worship* itself is from the old English term "worthship"—declaring the worth of God Himself! But while worship focuses on God's character, praise focuses on God's acts on our behalf. In this regard, Miriam's lyric embraces a bit of both:

And Miriam the prophetess, Aaron's sister, took the timbrel in her hand, and all the women went out after her with timbrels and with dancing. And Miriam answered them,

"Sing to the Lord, for He is highly exalted;
The horse and his rider He has hurled into the sea" (Exodus 15:20–21).

Note the element of worship in her first phrase, "Sing to the Lord, for He is highly exalted" and the praise and celebration in the second phrase, "The horse and his rider He has hurled into the sea." The anthem Miriam raised was full of cheer and rejoicing and thanksgiving. Imagine the scene. Exodus 15:20 says that Miriam led "all the women"—that would be hundreds of thousands of women uniting their voices, their musical instruments, and their dancing feet together to give praise and worship to the God of their rescue! Inspired and inspiring.

The best worship and praise music is music that focuses on who God is and what God does. I have been richly blessed over the years by music that "sings to the Lord, for He is highly exalted." Whether it is someone well-known like a Dámaris Carbaugh singing, "He Has Forgiven Me," or someone less-known, like Melissa Van Der Hulst (my favorite singer from my former church), singing "Cross of Love," there is something wonderful about the combination of sweetness and power in the voice of a woman singing praise to God. And, in some ways, all these worshiping women owe a debt to Miriam, prophetess and choir leader, who blazed the trail for them.

Tragic Acts of Spiritual Failure

The problem with heroes, of course, is that their heroism cannot perfectly overcome their humanity. Filled with human frailties, they, like us, find themselves living through the turmoil of life's inevitable ups and downs. Years ago I read a book on the life of Moses aptly titled *Moments of Glory: Feet of Clay* to describe the certainty of our human frailty and the very real possibility of our human failings. Even a courageous spiritual leader like Miriam could not fully escape these realities.

For years, since she was a young girl, Miriam had protected and supported her brother Moses. Now, however, we see her heart turn in a different direction—and a very negative one at that. Ninety years have passed since she was willing to risk her life for her brother, and now she has become jealous of him and those around him. Now, by her attitudes and activities late in her life, she lives down to the worst elements of her name, as, with the aid of her brother Aaron, Miriam attempts to undermine the leadership and ministry of Moses. In fact, it is possible that *Miriam* was not her birth name at all, but was a name given to her later to describe her character later in her life. Perhaps that is why, though she appears in the early narratives of the book of Exodus, she remains unnamed in the text until Exodus 15.

◆

One of the most popular game shows in television history was *Family Feud,* where members of two families would duke it out over trivial questions for cash. In real life, though, few things are as disheartening or unrewarding or just plain ugly as when families battle. Feuds between two families are as old as the Hatfields and McCoys or as Shakespeare's Capulets and Montagues. Family feuds almost always end tragically.

But as bad as it is when two families fight, it does not begin to approach the ugliness when the feuding is between members of the same family— something as old as Cain and Abel.

When I moved with my wife and four small children to the Los Angeles area to pastor a church, I learned how this could happen even in ministry. The church I was called to had been without a pastor for almost a year, and the congregation had dwindled from almost 500 in Sunday morning attendance to fewer than 150. They had lost millions of dollars in property (along with hundreds of thousands of dollars invested in that property) and a Christian school ministry. As I questioned the leadership regarding how they had gotten to that point, the answer was painful to hear. The previous two full-time pastors were brothers, and one brother had tried to have the other removed so he could be the lead pastor. Both men ended up leaving, and the church, or what remained of it, was shot through with division, polarized around the personalities of the departed brothers. No, family feuds are not pretty.

And that's what happened when Miriam's attitude toward her brother Moses became tainted by jealousy. Nor was she content to act alone. She enlisted the help of their brother Aaron and began a campaign to undermine Moses' leadership by attacking his character: "Miriam and Aaron spoke against Moses because of the Cushite woman whom he had married" (Numbers 12:1). Without doubt, Moses' decision to marry another woman was not the wisest thing he ever did! He had one wife—Zipporah, a Midianite—meaning that Moses now had one wife too many! Remember that, in the total honesty of Scripture, the Bible reveals even the failures and sins of God's people; but merely because the Bible records certain activities or attitudes does not mean the Bible endorses them! Moses' bigamy made him vulnerable to questions of character— questions that were raised not by political enemies, but by his own brother and sister!

As testimony to the ugliness of such intra-family struggles, Miriam did not enter the conflict armed with facts and truth, but with innuendo and sarcasm, all with one clear goal: to undermine Moses' leadership. The real reason for this attack was not Moses' wives, but Miriam's and Aaron's jealousy of Moses' personal relationship with God and what went with it—his place and standing in the community. Notice their self-driven words: "'Has the Lord indeed spoken only through Moses? Has He not spoken through us as well?' And the Lord heard it" (Numbers 12:2).

That last phrase is the kicker: "And the Lord heard it." Miriam and Aaron got more attention than they had bargained for! God heard their remarks, and His response was immediate and chastening.

God called the three siblings, all now at least in their nineties, to the tabernacle and began to describe His relationship with Moses. "My servant Moses, he is faithful in all My household; with him I speak mouth to mouth, even openly . . . and he beholds the form of the Lord." The Lord and His special servant Moses had a truly unique relationship: God spoke with Moses face-to-face. It seemed to be a relationship Miriam envied, but was a relationship she could not share, because Moses had been set aside for this unique place in God's plan.

The Lord asks, "Why then were you not afraid to speak against My servant, against Moses?" But Miriam's and Aaron's petty jealousies had resulted in an arrogance that negated any fear. And so God displayed His righteous anger against their contentious hearts.

Why such anger? Well, as the writer of Proverbs would later tell us, there are seven things that God hates and views as abominable, and one of those things is the "one who spreads strife among brothers" (Proverbs 6:19).

It seems clear that God considered Miriam the leader of, and the one most responsible for, this jealous and selfish rebellion, because she was the one He struck with His hand of judgment. "So the anger of the Lord burned against them and He departed. But when the cloud had withdrawn from over the tent, behold, Miriam was leprous, as white as snow" (Numbers 12:9–10).

In ancient times, leprosy was a terrifying disease. There was no cure, and the disease resulted in physical deterioration, social isolation, and, ultimately, death. Because of the great fear that any kind of contact could spread this death sentence to others, "lepers" were banished from the larger community and placed in leper colonies where they would not pose a threat to others. For these reasons, leprosy was also the quintessential picture of sin. Sin also destroys, isolates, and results in death—with no human remedy available. But as bad as leprosy was, Miriam's leprosy was even worse because it was a direct result of God's chastening. And as a further sign of His judgment, God cast her out of the Israelite camp for seven days.

Miriam had challenged Moses and attempted to unseat him as leader of the Israelite nation, yet he sought God's mercy on her behalf, pleading for Him to withdraw His chastening. Aaron also pleaded her cause. It is more than a little interesting that, while interceding for Miriam, Aaron also pleaded for forgiveness for his part in the rebellion. Tragically, Miriam made no such appeal. Whether because of the hardness of her heart or a misguided sense of self-justification, she did not acknowledge her sin and seek forgiveness. As a result, the Lord dealt firmly with Miriam and she was put out of the camp—set aside because of her rebellious spirit.

(Just as a side note, Miriam and Aaron were not the only Israelites to rebel against Moses' leadership. Others, like the sons of Korah, would also rebel against him [Numbers 16]. But when this disruption came from those closest to Moses, it had a different sting.)

For seven days Miriam was separated from the community of faith. This was not to "teach Miriam her place," but to help her understand her role. She was to support and encourage her brother and to help him in his massive task, not to jeopardize his mission. And God, in His perfect wisdom, knew there was only one way for Miriam to learn humility. Job learned humility and repentance through suffering and personal pain, and the apostle Paul learned grace the same way. Even Christ Himself, though He was the Son of God, "learned obedience through the things which He suffered" (Hebrews 5:8). Thus, Miriam learned lessons of humility through the suffering of God's judgment for her rebellion.

The Testimony of Silence

Normally an argument from silence is the weakest form of argument. In Miriam's life, however, silence speaks very loudly! Following her rebellion and chastening, Miriam is never mentioned again, except in the record of her death, which, sadly, is little more than a footnote in the history of Israel's wanderings. "Then the sons of Israel, the whole congregation, came to the wilderness of Zin in the first month; and the people stayed at Kadesh. Now Miriam died there and was buried there" (Numbers 20:1). We don't know how much time transpired between her rebellion and her death, but we do know that she is never again recognized as a leader in Israel.

Why did Miriam, who had so much to offer her people both in life experience and in leadership, spend the rest of her days in silence? Perhaps she was silent out of sorrow over her failure and lost testimony. Perhaps she was silent out of fear: having once experienced God's chastening, she was determined not to experience it again. Or possibly she was silent out of bitterness over God's defense of Moses and her loss of the influence.

We do not know. What we do know is that the influence she so desperately sought to enlarge was gone, and that she never saw the Promised Land. The only other time Miriam is mentioned in Scripture is in the book of the law when she is used as an example of being careful against the infection of leprosy: "Remember what the Lord your God did to Miriam on the way as you came out of Egypt" (Deuteronomy 24:9). What a painful, unfortunate ending to a life that began so courageously and selflessly.

◆

Miriam's life was more a crazy quilt than a formal portrait. Rarely in a "minor character" do we see such diversity of application, of examples both good and bad. Miriam showed courage and compassion in protecting her baby brother Moses, and loyalty and strength in supporting his leadership years later. She showed both a heart of worship and the skill of leadership as she sang in praise to God at the Red Sea. Yet, in contrast, she revealed great selfishness and jealousy in her power play against Moses. What a tragedy that Miriam's life, begun so well, ended up as an object lesson on leprosy.

Benedict Arnold was one of America's earliest revolutionary heroes, serving valiantly under George Washington in the Continental Army. At some point, however, Arnold turned away from his fledgling nation and became a spy for the enemy. Historians debate the reasons for his betrayal—disillusionment with the cause, desire for money, seduction by a woman are some of the reasons offered—but whatever his reason, when the names of the great patriots of the War for Independence are mentioned, we hear names like George Washington, Patrick Henry, Frances Marion, Betsy Ross, and Nathan Hale. Not Benedict Arnold. Instead, the view of a life once respected for its good deeds and even for its patriotism was changed forever by one bad choice.

So it was with Miriam. A name that could have, and perhaps should have, been associated with heroism and praise, with wisdom and worship, with honor and valor, became instead a watchword for isolation and divine chastening.

PRINCIPLES FROM THE LIFE OF MIRIAM

Despite the failure and silence at the end of her life, Miriam has many good things to teach us, and one of those good things is the joy of wholehearted worship.

- Worship is primarily vertical, focusing our attention on who God is rather than on what He does.

- Worship acknowledges and extols God's attributes by recognizing and celebrating His holiness and perfection.

- Worship eventually dissolves into praise as we recognize how God has worked on our behalf. In praise, we glorify the greatness of God's character as He has moved and worked on our behalf.

- Worship often involves musical expression but is not limited to it. Rather, the living of our lives is to be an ongoing expression of our worship of God.

- Worship is the language and primary activity of heaven, always giving glory to God.

8

Naomi

A Heart of Sorrow

I have had the opportunity to visit Israel several times, and one of the highlights and most unforgettable events of each trip have been my visits to Yad Vashem, the memorial to the millions of victims of the Holocaust, located in Jerusalem.

The Holocaust is one of the darkest episodes of atrocities and horror in human history, and when you enter Yad Vashem you sense the weight of this history. You are immediately struck by the somber atmosphere and the almost reverent silence as you visit the Children's Memorial, a tribute to the approximately 1.5 million Jewish children who perished during the Holocaust, where the names of murdered children, their ages, and their countries of origin can be heard being read continually in the background; the Historical Museum with its grim details and photographs; the Valley of the Communities, where the names and stories of over 5,000 Jewish communities that were destroyed are engraved into walls of bright white

Jerusalem stone—symbolically embedded forever in the bedrock of Jerusalem. These displays, and many more, point to and memorialize a time of evil and suffering that is in many ways unparalleled in modern experience. Yad Vashem is a fascinating, heartbreaking, infuriating place.

Like most people, I struggle with all of this. I struggle to understand the ugly hatred of human beings for other human beings. I struggle to understand the evil that could destroy human life as if it were refuse.

Yad Vashem always reminds me of the virulence of human hatred . . . but it also reminds me of the courage of the human heart, for another section at the memorial is the Avenue of the Righteous Among the Nations, which honors those known and unknown Gentiles, like Oskar Schindler and Corrie ten Boom, who risked or gave their own lives to save their Jewish friends, neighbors, or even those they did not know. And Yad Vashem reminds me of the resilience of the human heart, for out of the Holocaust was born the modern state of Israel. Suffering and celebration out of the same event. These are difficult things to understand and reconcile. And some people are never able to accept the tension of such extremely different emotions in one place.

Elie Weisel, the acclaimed author and Nobel Peace Prize winner, survived the death camps of Auschwitz, Buchenwald, and Birkenau. He lost most of his family in the camps, and witnessed more horror in his life than most of us can ever imagine, but the scars of his suffering are much more than just physical. In his first book, *Night,* he writes of his first night at Auschwitz:

> Never shall I forget that night, the first night in camp,
> which has turned my life into one long night, seven times

cursed and seven times sealed. Never shall I forget the smoke. Never shall I forget the faces of the children whose bodies I saw turned into wreaths of smoke beneath a silent blue sky. Never shall I forget those flames which consumed my faith forever.

Strong words. But I would advise against standing too harshly in judgment of Weisel's heart. Instead, we must look at the anger, frustration, and hurt that this terrible pain produced in him, and understand how easily such suffering can bear bitter fruit and consume someone's faith.

Weisel was not the first, nor will he be the last, to be embittered by the sufferings and injustices of life. In the Old Testament, all the way back to the years of the judges, another dark time in human history, we meet another person whose heart was turned hard and bitter by the events of life.

A Name That Mirrors a Heart

Her name was *Naomi*, which can be translated "pleasant," "my joy," or even the "pleasantness of Jehovah." It is a name that suggests all that is charming, agreeable, and attractive (Lockyer, *All the Women of the Bible*, 116). At a certain point in her life, however, she changed her name to Mara, which means "bitterness" (see also Exodus 15:23). What caused a woman initially marked out by the pleasant things of life to become so embittered by events and circumstances that she would actually change her name? Let's look at what happened.

When we are first introduced to Naomi and her family, she and her husband and their two sons have just moved to Moab because of a famine in their homeland of Bethlehem in Judah (Ruth 1). Her husband was Elimelech (which means "God is my king"), and he was the brother of Salmon a prince of Judah who had married Rahab, the woman of Jericho who had come to the aid of the Israelites when they were first spying out the Promised Land (Lockyer, 116). Theirs was a wealthy and prosperous family, meaning that Naomi had, for that time and place, married into a relatively comfortable lifestyle of material plenty. Besides that material plenty and the love of a husband, God blessed her with two sons, Mahlon and Chilion.

As we have noted throughout this book, and as we see in the Bible, names meant a great deal in ancient Israel. Names were chosen with care, purpose, and intent. But why Naomi and Elimelech chose these names for their two sons is a mystery, because Mahlon means "to cause grief and affliction," while Chilion means "to destroy and cause weeping." Why parents would give such names to their children is difficult to understand; yet, as it would turn out, these names became painfully appropriate.

Nonetheless, when we first meet her, Naomi's life is a mirror image of her name—full, happy, joyous. As so often happens, though, God tends to work at the point of our spiritual need. He taught Joseph to be a leader by bringing him into a season of servanthood. He taught David to rule men by allowing him to lead sheep. He taught Peter to learn dependence on God by teaching him the dangers of self-reliance. Naomi also needed to learn hard lessons. Certainly she was joyful, but was her joy linked to the plenty and pleasure of her life itself or to the God who had supplied it? What would happen if she lost everything, as Job had? Could she learn to be joyful with nothing, as she had been with everything?

God often runs us through the grid of testing to show us the weaknesses of our own heart. He did this with Naomi, too, and her life-view changed with her life-situation. This change from laughter to sorrow did not occur all at once, however, but through a series of circumstances that caused her downward slide into grief, despair, and bitterness.

FAMINE

It all began with a famine in Bethlehem (Ruth 1:1), which seems ironic, since the name Bethlehem means "house of bread." But there came a time when there was no more bread in Bethlehem, and no grain with which to make it. This famine had a purpose, however. It truly was an "act of God" because God was dealing with Israel's sin:

> "But if you do not obey Me, and do not observe all these commandments, and if you despise My statutes, or if your soul abhors My judgments, so that you do not perform all My commandments, but break My covenant, I also will do this to you: I will even appoint terror over you, wasting disease and fever which shall consume the eyes and cause sorrow of heart. And you shall sow your seed in vain, for your enemies shall eat it" (Leviticus 26:14–16 NKJV).

God had warned Israel that if they did not obey Him, they would sow their seed in vain. The results of such a judgment would be sweeping, particularly in an agrarian culture.

In the science fiction novel *No Blade of Grass* the world is stricken by a virus that destroys all the grasses—everything from Kentucky bluegrass to wheat to barley and even most forms of rice. Unable to grow food, people become desperate, and the impact on the world is devastating, creating every form of self-protection, including war and murder. The images of a world without grass are chilling. Thankfully it is just a novel.

For Elimelech and his family and neighbors famine was not fiction; it was the glaring reality of life. This was more than just hardship born out of the loss of physical and material comforts. It struck at the most basic human need—bread!

Why did God choose this method to confront Israel? Perhaps it was to remind them who their source of life really was. In the wilderness, Israel had learned to trust God every day for their daily bread (manna), but they had forgotten that powerful lesson in the Land of Promise. Fullness and plenty in a land flowing with milk and honey can cause spiritual amnesia; so much so that God must sometimes take away our ease to remind us that we are still dependent upon Him.

The famines of life—those dry and empty seasons of loss and despair—can pointedly refocus our values on the God of provision instead of on the provision itself. That is why Jesus said, "But seek first His kingdom and His righteousness, and all these things will be added to you" (Matthew 6:33). We must learn to seek Him first—and trust Him for the rest.

TRANSITION

Due to the severity of the famine, Elimelech moved his family from Bethlehem to Moab (Ruth 1:1–2). Moabite territory was only about thirty miles from Bethlehem, but it might as well have been on the dark side of the moon. This was Gentile, pagan territory and in this move they were:

- Abandoning roots and connections to hearth and home;
- Abandoning relationships with friends and loved ones;
- Abandoning the familiar and recognizable, and the relative comfort that goes with it;
- Abandoning their spiritual ties to the God of Israel, looking for answers to life's problems in a land of strange and foreign gods.

These are just a few of the reasons we fear change so very much. It upsets our applecart of "*status quo* living." I once heard a preacher say that "*status quo* is Latin for the mess we're in." In another comment on *status quo,* he said, "A rut is simply a grave with both ends knocked out." But our rut, our *status quo,* is comfortable, which is probably why we today define the pleasantness of the familiar as "comfort zones" and "comfort foods."

I have to admit that I am something of a fast-food junkie. I like burgers and fries and milkshakes and all that stuff that is not very good for me. In fact, I have developed something of a fondness for Krispy Kreme donuts, and a reputation to go with it—a reputation represented by the Krispy Kreme ball cap that proudly adorns my office. I know that an apple or a handful of grapes would be better for me, but, that's not my comfort food—my comfort food is usually something breaded and deep-fried (perhaps a lingering testimony to my southern upbringing). When I am traveling internationally, I usually seek out a McDonald's at some point during a long trip. As Os Guinness wrote, it is not because I am deceived into believing that "Big Mac" is necessarily the same thing as "Good Mac." It's because Mac is familiar. It tastes like home. It is comforting.

That is why transition and change can be tough to deal with. We find ourselves ripped from the familiar and comfortable, and faced with things that are odd and foreign. It's as if life itself has been turned on its side. This is the challenge of transition, even when there are good reasons for change. Change is about the unknown, and the unknown leaves us fearful and confused.

But the comforting truth is this: for God there is no unknown. For God there are no surprises. These truths are hard to remember in times of transition. But the stress that comes from change can be minimized when we do not allow transition to disrupt our trust in and dependence on the living God who fully knows the end from the beginning. In a sense, we can truly trust God in the *status quo* only if we are willing to let Him alter that *status quo*. We can fully accept and appreciate the normal only if we are open to the possibility of transition.

DISAPPOINTMENT

Naomi's *status quo* changed dramatically. Her status in life and her place of residence changed, and so did her family (Ruth 1:3–4).

Sometime after she and Elimelech settled in Moab—we're not told how long—Elimelech died. And sometime after that, both her sons met and married Gentile women, something the Israelites were warned against in the Mosaic law. This warning had been given by God because He knew that the Canaanite nations that would surround them in the Land of Promise were worshipers of multiple false gods, and by marrying into those tribal peoples, the Israelites would come under their pagan influence. This could—and did—cause Israel to shift their allegiance away from the God of Abraham, Isaac, and Jacob and give their affection, devotion, and worship to idols that could not hear them, love them, or answer their prayers. Such pagan influence had its effect for generations to come, perhaps finding its zenith in the days of King Ahab and his wife Jezebel a priestess of Baal (see chapter 3).

According to the traditional rabbinical teachings of Israel, Jewish parents had three duties to their sons:

- Teach them the law of Moses, in order to have a life built on truth;
- Give them a trade, in order to equip them for making a contribution to society;
- Find a suitable wife in order to carry on the family name.

These Gentile Moabite women did not fit the definition of "a suitable wife." They were women who were considered "out of bounds" for faithful men of God. Thus, Naomi faced what all parents fear: that our greatest pain and sorrow can come to us from our children.

Naomi's husband had died; her sons had gone astray. She was in a strange land, alone, disappointed, and deso-

143

late—living a life that rudely mocked her former days of joy.

Loss

Naomi had lost her husband to death and her sons to Moabite wives. But she soon faced even more heartache, for in the midst of her sadness over Elimelech's death and Mahlon's and Chilion's disappointing choices, her sons died (Ruth 1:3–5).

We don't know how much time elapsed between the weddings and the funerals, but it makes little difference. Pain is still pain, and there is something even more painfully unnatural about a parent burying a child. It simply isn't supposed to be that way. Children are supposed to bury their parents; that is the natural order of things. To bury your child is to bear the burden of the unthinkable.

What a tragic turn life had taken for Naomi. She had truly lost everything. From a life of comfort to a life of strangeness and suffering. From a home filled with love and joy to an empty house bereft of life. Burt Bacharach and Hal David, in one of their many popular songs, attempted to put such emptiness into words when they wrote, "A house is not a home when there's no one there to hold you tight." Naomi's experience painfully matches the isolation of those words. Everywhere she looked she not only saw the aloneness of her empty home—she felt it. No one there.

"Would a loving God do that?" "Why does such pain have to assault us in the depths of our hearts?" These questions scream for an answer. Yet in this life we are unable to find full or satisfying answers apart from the answer of trust in a God who makes no mistakes, a God who loves us and cares for us, even when we hurt and don't know why.

Job's response to the problem of pain and suffering was one of trust, even when he had no answers for his struggling questions: "'Naked I came from my mother's womb, and naked I shall return there. The Lord gave and the Lord has taken away. Blessed be the name of the Lord.' Through all this Job did not sin nor did he blame God" (Job 1:21–22).

Naomi's response was very different from Job's. It was both more harsh and more typically human: "I went out full, but the Lord has brought me back empty. Why do you call me Naomi, since the Lord has witnessed against me and the Almighty has afflicted me?" (Ruth 1:21).

Naomi's attitude was more about bitterness than about trust, more about self-pity than about faith. On a human level, it is certainly understandable. In the midst of her grief, she had plenty of justification for her feelings. She needed a clearer view of how much God loved her. Hebrews 12:5–11 declares that God's love for His child is so intense, so severe, so sweeping that even chastening is evidence of the Father's love in our lives. Evidence of love, not the opposite of it! But Naomi was not able to see this, nor to trust God's love. Her spiritual vision had been blurred by tears and grief.

So the woman who left Bethlehem full of hope and life now decides to return home to Bethlehem without sons or husband, bitter against God and against life, with nothing to show for her years of pain and loss but two Gentile daughters-in-law, Orpah and Ruth.

A Life That Needs Hope

In J. R. R. Tolkien's classic trilogy *The Lord of the Rings,* we are drawn into a fantasy tale of the conflict between good and evil. The focus of this story is the battle for the ring of power and the fellowship of residents of Middle Earth who set out on a journey to destroy the ring and end the power of the evil Sauron. Powerful spiritual lessons are implicit throughout Tolkien's masterpiece, but one that is often overlooked comes near the end of the story, when it seems that the power of evil is about to overcome them. As two members of the fellowship, Gimli (the dwarf) and Legolas (the elf) prepare for the epic battle that could well determine the future of the world of men, they suddenly realize that the journey of struggle, loss, and hardship has brought them something special: friendship. If they must die in battle, they will at least die at the side of a friend; and in that both find great comfort and encouragement in a time when all seems dark and lost.

In the midst of her own battle with bitter loss, Naomi had also gained a significant blessing, but she did not yet realize it. She, too, had been blessed with a friend from the most unlikely of sources. None other than Ruth, her Moabitess daughter-in-law!

True friends are friends of the heart—those whose devotion, compassion, care, and concern for us outweigh their concern for themselves. Many people find themselves fortunate to have one or two true friends in a lifetime. Some don't have even that. They live much of their lives in isolation, feeling alone in a crowd. Perhaps this is true because we often view friendship through the wrong end of the telescope. Instead of entering into a friendship to see what we can give or what we can do for another person, our tendency is to measure and weigh the value of a relationship by what we can gain from it. To have friends you must first of all show yourself to be friendly, says the proverb (Proverbs 18:24 KJV). We cannot be self-centered and full of self-pity if we want real friends, because that attitude will prevent us from giving ourselves away. Christ Himself expressed the depth of this when He said, "Greater love has no one than this, that one lay down his life for his friends" (John 15:13).

The point is simple: you have to be willing to give of yourself to be a friend. Naomi's daughter-in-law Ruth had already learned this, and we see in her example the true comfort and encouragement that friendship brings.

◆

In her emptiness and loss, Naomi prepared to return to Bethlehem in an attempt to find comfort and an escape from the land of her grief. As she began to leave, her daughters-in-law offered to go with her, but she refused them. They were young and had at least the possibility of a future; she was worn down and broken by life. Additionally, it could be very difficult explaining these pagan daughters-in-law to her remaining friends and family back home in Bethlehem. No, it would be better for everyone involved if the young women remained in their own land with their own people, and Naomi urged them to do so.

One daughter-in-law, Orpah, turned back, but not the other. Ruth was determined to care for the mother of her late husband, and she responded with words of compassion, commitment, and care.

"Entreat me not to leave you, or to turn back from following after you; for wherever you go, I will go; and wherever you lodge, I will lodge; your people shall be my people, and your God, my God. Where you die, I will die, and there will I be buried. The Lord do so to me, and more also, if anything but death parts you and me" (Ruth 1:16–17 NKJV).

Ruth's intentions were clear. She intended to make the people of Naomi her people.

Without question, Naomi had suffered much and lost much, but she had also gained something precious in the friendship of a beloved daughter-in-law. Her veil of pain was beginning to lift, and the daughter-in-law who would accompany her to Bethlehem was now also a sister of faith, having not only embraced Naomi's family, but her God as well.

A Result That Builds Faith

Ruth now takes the spotlight, but her life choices are to have a great impact on Naomi's life. Once she and Naomi are back in Bethlehem, Ruth meets Boaz, a significant member of the community, and becomes his wife (Ruth 2–4). The result is blessing to Naomi! She could not see beyond the borders of her own world of pain, but God's sovereignty knows no such boundaries. Neither Bethlehem nor Moab could contain His workmanship.

Who would have ever guessed that God would give Naomi the family she longed for through Ruth, the Moabitess widow of her son, and Boaz, the near kinsman of their family? If there is a lesson in this it may be that we should never underestimate God. He is much more creative than you or I could ever imagine!

Naomi's bitterness turns to joy as God fills the emptiness of her life with the replenishment of a heritage and the joy of a role to fulfill. Like Job, her life is more full after the season of trials than it ever was when she thought she had it all.

> So Boaz took Ruth and she became his wife; and when he went in to her, the Lord gave her conception, and she bore a son. Then the women said to Naomi, "Blessed be the Lord, who has not left you this day without a near kinsman, and may his name be famous in Israel! And may he be to you a restorer of life and a nourisher of your old age; for your daughter-in-law, who loves you, who is better to you than seven sons, has borne him."
>
> Then Naomi took the child and laid him on her bosom, and became a nurse to him. Also the neighbor women gave him a name, saying, "There is a son born to Naomi." And they called his name Obed. He is the father of Jesse, the father of David (Ruth 4:13–17 NKJV).

Out of Naomi's time of desolation came a season of emptiness. But then God gave an Obed, then a Jesse, and ultimately a David! What a reminder of the truthfulness of the Word of God: "And we know that God causes all things to work together for good to those who love God . . . " (Romans 8:28).

For Naomi, change produced bitterness, which was an understandable but wrong response. Yet through her experience we see that we really can trust God in all things. Even in the bitterest of change, disappointment, and loss we need not become bitter. Even in the midst of fear there is hope. He really does know what He is doing. We can trust and rest in Him.

One man wrote, "We can respond to evil in our lives because we know that God is all-good and all-powerful—because we know Jesus." Erwin Lutzer, pastor of the Moody Memorial Church in Chicago, agreed with that idea, expressing it this way:

> This is the trial of our faith. Jesus has come to reveal the Father to us. And through Him we know that God sees how much we are able to endure while we continue to believe He knows best. When God chooses to do the opposite of what we think a God of love should do, that is a test of our loyalty. Jesus comforts us, "Do not let your hearts be troubled. Trust in God; trust also in Me." Blessed is the person who understands we must trust God's heart when we cannot understand God's hand; blessed is the person who knows that we must stand in awe in the presence of the mystery of God's purposes. Blessed is the person who goes on believing in God no matter what. Blessed is the person who lets God be God.

Faith is a matter of trust, and each of us, in the crucible of suffering, must make the call: Will we let God be God and trust Him, resting in His wisdom and goodness, no matter what? Or will we trust Him only when He is giving us our heart's desires? Your answer determines whether you are willing to let Him be God, or whether you demand that role for yourself.

> God moves in a mysterious way
> His wonders to perform;
> He plants His footsteps in the sea
> And rides upon the storm.

150

Deep in unfathomable mines
Of never-failing skill
He treasures up His bright designs
And works His sovereign will.

You fearful saints, fresh courage take;
The clouds you so much dread
Are big with mercy and shall break
In blessings on your head.

Judge not the Lord by feeble sense,
But trust Him for His grace;
Behind a frowning providence
He hides a smiling face.

His purposes will ripen fast,
Unfolding every hour;
The bud may have a bitter taste,
But sweet will be the flower.

Blind unbelief is sure to err
And scan His work in vain;
God is His own interpreter,
And He will make it plain.
                    —William Cowper

Will you trust Him—and let God be God? Will you allow your pain to drive you to His sheltering, everlasting arms of love—or away from His comforting and sustaining grace? The lesson Naomi learned can be an example for each of us in our own times of struggle: it is always the right time to trust in the purposes of our loving heavenly Father!

We cannot see beyond the horizon, but God can.

PRINCIPLES FROM THE LIFE OF NAOMI

♦ In times of blessing we need to focus on the God of provision, not the provision of God.

♦ The stability of Christ can calm our troubled hearts in times of transition, change, and fear of the unknown.

♦ The character of a true friend is the character of a giver, and that kind of friend, in itself, is one of the greatest gifts we can receive. (A true friend is a gift from God. Who are you God's gift to?)

♦ Allow the creativity of God to surprise you. He can provide and deliver in ways that are beyond imagination.

♦ Even in the most difficult times of life we can be confident in the never-failing goodness of God.

9

Philip

An Available Man

Timing can be everything. If you don't believe me, consider Lou Gehrig.

In 1925 the New York Yankees had a good first baseman with the promise of a long career. His name was Wally Pipp. One day Pipp sat out the game because of a headache, and a young, unknown backup, Lou Gehrig, took his place. The result was that Gehrig became baseball's original "Iron Man," playing for the next thirteen years in 2,130 consecutive games (a record that stood for almost six decades before it was broken by Cal Ripken, Jr. of the Baltimore Orioles) before being struck down with ALS, now often referred to as "Lou Gehrig's Disease." Wally Pipp never became a regular for the Yankees again, and his name is not often remembered today. Timing.

By contrast, look at Brian Griese. After a highly successful college football career at the University of Michigan that showed him to have talent, promise, and potential, Griese went to the NFL's Denver Broncos. The expectations at Denver were high, to say the least. Griese's predecessor was John Elway, perennial All-Pro and future Hall of Fame quarterback who had led the Broncos to two Super Bowl victories. With such high expectations, Griese seemingly never had a chance. After several years in Denver, during which his performance could generously be described as "adequate," Griese found himself dispensable and ultimately went to Miami, only to apparently serve as a backup quarterback there. He has since moved on again. Timing.

And what about Ronald Reagan or Jimmy Carter? Carter had the misfortune of inheriting an economic nightmare and a national crisis of trust. He also happened to be the sitting president when the Iran hostage crisis occurred. Few things so completely picture the significance of timing as one-term president Jimmy Carter watching powerless as the Iranian hostage crisis came to an end just as Ronald Reagan was being sworn into office as his successor. Reagan went on to become a popular two-term president during a time of economic upturn, the ending of the Cold War, and renewed patriotic fervor. Timing.

What a difference it makes to be the right person in the right place at the right time—or the wrong person in the wrong place at the wrong time. Timing can be everything.

When I went to college the second time (long story) at age twenty-one, I attended a new, small Christian college. Today, that school has a student body that numbers in the thousands, but then it was in the hundreds. The result was a very shallow talent pool and, consequently, numerous opportunities for people of questionable ability—like myself. I had opportunities in athletics, drama, academics, and ministry that today at the school would probably go to someone more gifted. Fortunately for me, I was there when the talent pool was not quite so deep. Timing.

Another person who was the right man for the right job at the right time was a man named Philip, and the God of providence, for whom there are no coincidences, used him mightily in the early spread of the gospel.

An Available Man

As we begin, it is important to identify just which Philip we are talking about here, because several "Philips" are mentioned in the New Testament. The name *Philip* had become popular in the ancient world because of the historic esteem in which Philip of Macedon, the father of Alexander the Great and founder of the Greek Empire, was held. As a result, particularly among those of Grecian descent, Philip was a very attractive name.

One such Philip was the brother of Herod. This Philip was the provisional ruler of the Galilean region of Judea during the first century. Another Philip was one of our Lord's disciples. He became a disciple early in Jesus' earthly ministry and brought Nathanael into the apostolic band (John 1:43–44). Philip was faithful to the Savior and was with the disciples in the upper room following Jesus' ascension to heaven (Acts 1).

The Philip we want to consider, however, steps onto the scene later than both of these, and we first see him mentioned during a crucial time in the early days of the early church (Acts 6). At this time, the church was struggling with division in the fellowship of believers because of a perceived inequity in the ministry to help widows.

In the early church, believers pooled their resources to care for those who had no means of support, and it seemed to some that the Jewish widows who were native to Palestine were being treated with favoritism over the Hellenistic Jewish widows (Jewish widows who were originally from Greece). Having already seen imprisonment and persecution from without, the leadership of the Jerusalem church now had to deal with conflict from within. Though such problems may seem relatively insignificant when compared to imprisonment, persecution, and death, they are the typical kind of struggles a growing congregation faces. With the burgeoning church family came a vast number of new responsibilities, caring ministries, and leadership tasks—a situation not conducive to trying to maintain focus on a teaching ministry that would have significance.

Their decision? Select a group of men to oversee the management of the widows' ministry.

Two things stand out about the men who were chosen. First, they are described in terms of their spiritual character. The apostles made it clear that character was the primary qualification when they chose these men, who are believed by many to be the first "deacons" of the church. Those qualifications included having a good reputation, being filled with the Holy Spirit, and being filled with wisdom (Acts 6:3). The apostles wanted these men to be trustworthy and fair in their dealings with the widows of the church and to be perceived as such.

The second notable characteristic of these men is that they all had Greek names: Prochorus, Nicanor, Timon, Parmenas, Nicolas, Stephen, and Philip (Acts 6:5). What great wisdom on the part of the leaders of the church. Because the concern about mistreatment came from those of

Greek background, men with some level of Greek background were selected to see that there was no inequity in that ministry. And one of those men was Philip, who was not only the right man in the right place at the right time, but was a man willing to be available for service. Though some might have viewed the widows' ministry as a matter of secondary importance, Philip seems to have willingly stepped in when given the opportunity, and he served faithfully and honorably in that position.

This is a valuable reminder. Just as there are no insignificant people in the body of Christ, so there are no insignificant ministries if they are performed in Jesus' name. Had Philip been driven by ambition or personal achievement, he could have held out for a more "important" role in ministry. He did not, however. He served in the role given him and made the most of it. He was an available man in the right place at the right time.

Bobby Michaels is a Christian vocal soloist with whom I've had the privilege of ministering at Bible conferences. Bobby once told me of a time in the mid-to-late 1980s when he was in a planning session with some of the other leading Christian artists of the day and noticed a young intern attending the meetings. The intern's role was to get the coffee, clean up after the meeting, and generally stay out of everyone's way. At the conclusion of the meeting, another participant asked Bobby how his current album project was coming together. When he replied that he needed one more song to finish the album, his friend pointed to the intern and said, "The kid cleaning up the table is writing some interesting stuff. Why don't you talk to him?"

Bobby did, and the young man wrote the final song for his album. The song was entitled "My Redeemer Is Faithful and True," and the young intern was Steven Curtis Chapman, who has since become one of the most successful Christian singer/songwriters of the last fifteen years.

Imagine if Chapman had felt that the intern job was beneath him. Being in that room, getting the coffee and cleaning up after the meeting, put him in position for what would become a major breakthrough for his musical career and ministry. He was available—and in God's perfect timing, that availability meant a life-changing opportunity.

The same was true of Philip. He accepted the opportunity presented to him and served, and that service created a training ground for his future ministry as well as a proving ground for his own humility and availability. Philip embraced a ministry to the forgotten, and his faithfulness was not forgotten by God.

A Useful Man

Because of the training ground of the widows' ministry, Philip was strategically positioned to move forward in spiritual service. In a sense, he became the poster child for the spiritual maxim, "Faithful in a few things, ruler over many things." The key, of course, is that he did not enter into the widows' ministry because it was a good career move that would vault him into the spotlight. He did it because it needed to be done, and his faithful ministry did not go unrecognized.

As the gospel began to spread throughout the Palestine of the first century, it found its way into Samaria (Acts 8). But this spiritual incursion into Samaria raised some concerns. Samaria was the region between Galilee in the north and Judea in the south, and was inhabited by an ethnic group that was utterly despised by the Jewish people. This animosity dated back hundreds of years. The Samaritans were the descendants of Jews who had been left behind when the southern kingdom had been taken into captivity in Babylon six hundred years before. Those who remained in Judah intermarried with the Gentiles of the area, and their descendants were despised because of their lack of "ethnic purity."

Jesus, of course, battled long and hard against such prejudice and bigotry. When traveling to Jerusalem during one part of His ministry, instead of following the normal Jewish custom of the day and heading south by way of the east side of the Jordan River to avoid the area of Samaria, Jesus went through Samaria (John 4). There He encountered a Samaritan woman at a well in the city of Sychar, a woman with deep spiritual needs and great personal pain. Jesus violated social mores when He spoke to her, but her spiritual well-being mattered more to Him than placating the prejudices of others.

In another case, Jesus shocked and stunned His religious audience by telling perhaps His greatest parable, a story in which two Jewish religious leaders became the villains and a Samaritan was the hero (Luke 10:30 ff.). The parable of "The Good Samaritan" was not only a declaration by Christ of what constituted a good neighbor, but also a revelation of the weaknesses of a heart governed by racial bigotry. And the bottom line of Jesus' message was that Jesus Christ fully intended to die for both Jew and Gentile—and Samaritan.

In the early church that racial barrier would again be breached (Acts 8). Following Stephen's execution, a time of intense persecution of the church began in Jerusalem, resulting in a mass exodus of believers from that city into any safe haven they could find. As they fled, they took the message of the cross with them and shared the gospel wherever they went.

Philip was one of those affected by this dispersion, and he became a preacher of great power as he went to Samaria to preach the gospel of Jesus Christ to the despised Samaritans. Since Philip was Greek, he was a good choice to minister to the "hated half-breeds" of Samaria. They would not view him with distrust and disregard as they might a Jewish spokesperson—again, the right man in the right place at the right time.

To be able to cross ethnic and racial barriers with the grace of Christ is not as easy as it sounds. Both sides carry presuppositions, whether accurate or inaccurate, about the other. Both sides have nagging doubts, even fears, about the other. Both sides carry a certain amount of baggage based on what they have felt, heard, seen, experienced, or supposed. And fighting through all that emotional baggage is only part of the problem. A person must first be willing to commit to the fight.

I grew up in the South and am painfully aware of the problems of racial tension. I also grew up in a home that was virtually color-blind. I watched my father as he interacted seamlessly and effortlessly with people of various racial backgrounds and I marveled at his heart. He spent the last years of his working life training, equipping, and finding jobs for some of the poverty-stricken people of Appalachia, regardless of their ethnic origins. It was a great lesson for me in what the heart of Christ looks like.

Years later I had the opportunity to pastor a small church in southern California that wonderfully and vividly resem-

bled the body of Christ. We had some measure of represen-
tation from many people groups—whites, blacks, Hispan-
ics, Asians, Middle-Easterners, and Polynesians. Some of
the greatest joys of that ministry, frankly, were the potluck
suppers, which were amazing international smorgasbords.
Authentic. Delicious. Wonderful. More important, however, was the privilege to be in a ministry where race was not
an issue of contention. For my family and me that ministry
experience was both an enormous personal blessing and a
breath of fresh air. I have to believe that Philip, who with
warm heart and open hand went to the Samaritans with
the love of Jesus, would have felt right at home in that little
church.

Remember, some Samaritans had already come to Jesus
through the ministry the Lord Himself had initiated with
the woman at the well of Sychar. These people were prepared to hear the gospel, and when Philip spoke to them
of the Jesus who had visited them years before, they responded. God greatly blessed Philip's heart and his ministry, and the results of God's wonderful work are found in
Acts 8:6–17:

- People believed the message of Christ. Philip entered
  a city in Samaria and declared God's salvation to the
  people. Their reaction was a preacher's dream come
  true. They listened attentively and then followed
  through with commitment in baptism (v. 12).
- The entire city was impacted by the changed lives.
  God blessed Philip's ministry with power, and the
  result was life-changing. People were healed. Hearts
  were changed. Eternities were radically altered. The

writer of Acts states yet understates well the impact of the gospel on the city by simply saying, "And there was great joy in that city" (Acts 8:8 KJV).

• The apostles validated Philip's ministry. The church at Jerusalem sent Peter and John to examine Philip's ministry to the Samaritans and to determine its faithfulness to the gospel. Their hearty endorsement underlined the undeniable reality of God's mighty work in that rather unlikely place. That endorsement even resulted in their own preaching in the villages of Samaria on their way back to Jerusalem (v. 25). Peter and John didn't merely observe—they joined in!

Timing. Yes, Philip was the right man in the right place at the right time, and he was there because he made himself available. His stage of preparation was his ministry with the widows of Jerusalem; this, combined with his unique background and credentials, gave him powerful influence in Samaria. Beyond that, the simple fact is that God mightily used Philip in effective ministry because Philip was useful. In heart, mind, spirit, and willingness, he was a prepared instrument in the hands of God for this significant work.

A Flexible Man

As someone whose adult life has been devoted to the preaching of the Bible, I have to confess to doing some head-scratching here. As I've said, the scene in Acts 8 is the preacher's dream come true. God was at work. Lives were being changed. Ministry was being effective. Joy was being embraced. It really doesn't get any better than this if you are a preacher.

Now, however, in the midst of this great moving of God when many people were coming to Christ, God called Philip to leave all that success and preach to only one man! In Acts 8:26–40 we see this improbable turn in the story:

> An angel of the Lord spoke to Philip saying, "Get up and go south to the road that descends from Jerusalem to Gaza." (This is a desert road.) So he got up and went; and there was an Ethiopian eunuch, a court official of Candace, queen of the Ethiopians, who was in charge of all her treasure; and he had come to Jerusalem to worship. And he was returning and sitting in his chariot, and was reading the prophet Isaiah. Then the Spirit said to Philip, "Go up and join this chariot" (Acts 8:26–29).

THE TARGET

The "Ethiopian eunuch," as he is usually called, was a spiritually lost man. In this passage he is described as a eunuch, which does not seem to be a sexual term here, but rather a reference to a religious advisor who was an influential court official for Candace, queen of Ethiopia. This man was a spiritual seeker and had come to Jerusalem to worship. Apparently his search had not been satisfied because he was still seeking answers, and he was seeking those answers in a fascinating place—by reading the prophet Isaiah.

The Ethiopian truly had a prepared heart. Yet even as prepared as this man was to hear the message of Christ, Philip faced several problems in dealing with him. He faced:

- Racial differences. One man was Ethiopian; the other was Greek in background.
- Social differences. The Ethiopian was a political adviser to a prominent person; Philip was a simple preacher, viewed by the world as insignificant.
- Spiritual differences. The Ethiopian was lost; Philip was a redeemed follower of Christ.

First Corinthians 2:14 tells us that the natural man cannot understand the things of the Spirit of God, for they are spiritually discerned. It should be no surprise, then, that this seeker was confounded as he attempted to study the book of Isaiah, one of the most theologically complex passages in the entire Old Testament. Yet Romans 1 tells us that God's glory is revealed everywhere in His creation, and if someone responds to that light, God will give greater light—the light of the gospel. The Ethiopian was a true seeker, and God sent a messenger to him who would bring him greater light.

THE MESSENGER

When Philip stepped into the chariot to share the message of Christ with this true seeker, his approach was basic and very sound. "Philip ran up and he heard him reading Isaiah the prophet, and said, 'Do you understand what you are reading?' And he said, 'Well, how could I, unless someone guides me?' And he invited Philip to come up and sit with him" (Acts 8:30–31).

Back to the basics is almost always a sound strategy. Football coaches drill their teams with the basics. Players like the flash of long pass plays, exciting kick returns, and slashing running schemes. Coaches know better, however. They know that football games are won by the basics— blocking and tackling. Blocking and tackling. Blocking and tackling. In the same way, Philip had a very basic strategy. It included:

- The right attitude. Philip was willing to be flexible. He was willing to adjust from the crowds of Samaria to the individual man in the desert. Some preachers can speak to great crowds, and some evangelists can share the gospel with one person. Philip was agile enough to be effective in both arenas.
- The right question. Philip established a point of contact with the man by making a connection with the right question: "Do you understand what you are reading?" he asked. The Ethiopian's obvious interest in the Scriptures was that connection.
- The right message. Philip preached Jesus to the Ethiopian! He didn't discuss philosophy or argue theology. He simply spoke of the Savior to a heart hungry for the Bread of Life.

This is not a terribly complicated pattern, and that is why it is so useful and effective. It is a basic pattern that we can implement as we reach out with the gospel to seeking hearts.

- Attitude: flexibility, compassion, concern, and humility.
- Ask questions: the Evangelism Explosion model is a practical place to start. That model flows from basically two spiritual questions that serve as "ice break-

ers." The first is, "If you were to die right now, would you go to heaven?" The second is, "If you stood before God and He asked you, 'Why should I let you into My heaven?' what would your answer be?"

- Answer from the Word: share the gospel. As people respond to gentle, appropriate questions, the heart-satisfying answers of the Bible can be offered.

Ultimately, though, what made Philip effective in evangelism was not his technique but his obedience. Like him, we must be faithful and obedient, allowing the grace and love of Jesus Christ to break down the walls of racial barriers, social strata, caste systems, and religious debate. When we do this, we may be privileged to introduce Christ to needy hearts.

THE MESSAGE

During one of my trips to Israel our group visited the fascinating site of Caesarea Philippi. It was there that Jesus asked His disciples, "Who do you say that I am?" to which Peter responded, "You are the Christ the Son of the living God."

Our Israeli guide gave us the history of the site, and then I taught from Matthew 16 about Jesus questioning His disciples. Usually after sharing the history of a site, the guides will drift away from the group. They hear Bible teachers and tour group leaders speaking of these things all the time, and, because they are Jewish, most have little interest in the message of Jesus. This time, however, I was surprised to see our guide stay by my side as I taught. When I was finished and the group broke away to take pictures, she stayed, obviously thinking about what she had just heard. When I asked her what she was thinking, she said, "I have led groups here for years, but have never heard this before. Could I ask you some questions?" It was then my great joy to sit with her and, with Bible open, discuss the person of Jesus Christ. Philip must have felt that same joy as he shared with the man from Ethiopia.

◆

Isaiah wrote prophetically of Jesus, the God-man. "The eunuch answered Philip and said, 'Please tell me, of whom does the prophet say this? Of himself, or of someone else?'" (Acts 8:34). In response to the Ethiopian's question, Philip walked him through the meaning and implications of these Old Testament prophecies of the suffering Savior that had been fulfilled in the coming of the Lord Jesus Christ.

Philip told him of the Savior, then called him to the obedience of faith in Christ. And the man accepted those words of life and love and grace! "As they went down the road, they came to some water. And the eunuch said, 'See, here is water. What hinders me from being baptized?' Then Philip said, 'If you believe with all your heart, you may.' And he answered and said, 'I believe that Jesus Christ is the Son of God'" (Acts 8:36–37 NKJV).

Jesus' death purchased forgiveness of sins, and His resurrection gave eternal life, but for the Ethiopian eunuch this salvation brought the wonderful dimension of life in Christ that we can never hear too much about—joy!

"When they came up out of the water, the Spirit of the Lord snatched Philip away; and the eunuch no longer saw him, but went on his way rejoicing" (Acts 8:39).

167

Philip had brought the joy of gospel to the Ethiopian eunuch, just as he had brought the joy of the power of the cross to Samaria (Acts 8:8).

Then, even as the Ethiopian was celebrating the wonder of God's grace, Philip departed as quickly as he had come—on his way to somewhere else to tell someone else the same powerful, life-changing message. This is the beauty of how God works in bringing people to the Savior:

One person has a need.

Another person has the solution.

God brings them together and produces His result.

◆

We can learn much from Philip's life and ministry pattern and from his passion. Philip was the right person in the right place at the right time. He was useful, flexible, and available.

Christ has Philips all over the world, and has since the church began. I have a pastor friend in Russia who is a Philip. He is passionate, committed, and, more than anything else, he is available for the work of God—so available that, at one point, he was planting churches in six villages at the same time. Every day he was in a different village, sharing the gospel, ministering to hearts, displaying the compassion of Christ. The seventh day each week he spent at home with his family. Vladimir seemed to me to be tireless, but it was not adrenaline or the desire for success that motivated him. It was a deep longing to be an instrument in the hands of God. It was an intentional determination to be available.

PRINCIPLES FROM THE LIFE OF PHILIP

◆ To be available, we need the right attitude: flexibility to adjust to the opportunities God presents us.

◆ To be available, we need the right obedience: as Isaiah said, we should echo, "Here am I, send me."

◆ To be available, we need the right message: not secondary issues, pet peeves, or human traditions, but Jesus Christ, crucified and risen.

◆ To be available, we need the right confidence: the effectiveness of our ministry is not based on our skill or winsomeness, but on the fact that God will do His work.

10

Sarah

THE LAUGHER

Safety tips are often useful. Like, "Turn off the electricity before you work on a light fixture" (which more than once I have forgotten to do—the real reason my hair is gray). Or, "Keep your hands out of the sink when running the garbage disposal," or "Don't use a cell phone while you're driving." (Okay, I confess that I often ignore that one.) However, using the car phone seems tame compared to the things I've seen drivers doing on the freeways of southern California (applying makeup, reading the newspaper, and eating a bowl of cereal—or all three at the same time!).

Still, safety tips, no matter how absurdly obvious, are there for a reason: to protect us from carelessness or danger. They warn us where the danger is and keep us safe from harm.

Back in the 1970s, singer-songwriter Jim Croce offered his listeners a helpful safety tip when he sang about Jim, the toughest of the tough guys on Chicago's rowdy South Side. As Croce described him, Jim was to be feared, respected, and avoided at all costs. When facing "the baddest man in town," Croce advised, "Don't mess around with Jim."

Wisdom says that you don't mess around with danger, no matter what form it takes. To ignore such advice can bring misfortune and, often, failure. This is doubly true in the spiritual realm. Remember who we are and who God is. As dramatist Alex Bradford warns, "Your arms are too short to box with God."

The Bible is full of spiritual safety tips to help us guard our hearts as we walk with God in a fallen world filled with potential disaster. To ignore these gracious warnings is not only to forget who we are, but to ignore who God is. One that is especially dangerous to ignore is: "Never, ever, laugh at God." This warning may strike you as blatantly obvious. Laugh at God? Who would ever do such a thing? Yet, one woman we meet in the Bible did precisely that— she actually laughed at God! And that error in judgment affected her entire life as well as the lives of others, even to this day.

A Woman with a History

Her name was *Sarai,* a name God later changed to *Sarah.* Both names carry the basic meaning of "princess," but the original form also suggested a person who was "contentious" or "quarrelsome," while the second form, *Sarah,* the feminine form of the Hebrew word *sar,* meant "commander," implying one who "ruled" (Lockyer, *All the Women of the Bible,* 155). The original form of her name possibly indicated her dominating personality, while the form conferred by God expressed her role as mother of the nation of descendants that He had promised to Abraham.

171

Sarai was a princess in a wealthy, prominent family in Ur of the Chaldees, a city in the Fertile Crescent of the Mesopotamia Valley, the ancient cradle of civilization—the region of the Middle East we today know as Iraq (Genesis 11:29–31; 20:12). Her father, Terah, was also the father of her husband Abram. Such family alliances of half-brothers and sisters were common in ancient cultures, a means by which to maintain pure bloodlines. We are told in Genesis 12:4 that Abram was seventy-five years old when he and Sarai did as God directed and left their home in Haran to begin their long journey to the Land of Promise (Canaan). Apparently Sarai was only ten years younger than Abram, which means that neither of them was young when they embarked on the greatest adventure of their lives.

For many years Sarai's marriage and home life seem to have been peaceful, but difficult days were ahead. Some of this difficulty came from the hardships of life in a nomadic culture, and some of the tensions and problems resulted, as we shall see, from Sarai's great beauty (certainly no fault of hers). But there is more. As I look at the home of Abram and Sarai, I sense more emptiness than fullness; and emptiness can produce contentiousness rather than contentment, quarreling instead of quietness, and resignation rather than reconciliation.

As we explore the flashpoints for stress in their home and marriage, it is vital that we understand the environment in which Abram and Sarai lived. This was not a world in which women pursued careers or achievements outside the home. It was a world in which motherhood was a woman's happiness and fulfillment. Though beautiful, wealthy, and married to a prominent man—a life many would covet—Sarai suffered the emptiness of a home

172

without children in a world where children were expected, and their childlessness became the source of her deepest frustration and disappointment. As her story unfolds, this becomes tragically clear.

A Woman of Great Beauty

Sarai was an attractive woman, and not only in her husband's eyes (Genesis 12:11, 14). Abram called her beautiful, but so did travelers who met the couple during their journey to Canaan. Her beauty was not marred by the passing of time nor by the strenuous and taxing nomadic life she and Abram endured in the Middle Eastern desert, today referred to as the Negev. Though the northern region of Canaan, later to be known as the Galilee, had seasons of the year when it was lush and green, the southern regions were arid and brown. Coupled with the difficulties of travel in that world, these environmental realities could easily have been expected to wear away at her beauty, but apparently they did not. Sarai's physical beauty was, if nothing else, resilient in the face of such a lifestyle.

When my wife and I were in college, but not yet married, we traveled across the country as part of a summer musical ministry team. It was a large group of seventy-five to eighty college kids, and, not surprisingly, some of us were already "couples," including Marlene and me. At the start of that forty-two-day tour there were six engaged couples on board the big Greyhound bus. At the end of the trip, only two engagements had survived.

Traveling together in such close quarters can be brutally eye-opening. You live on the bus. You eat on the bus. You sleep on the bus (no fun at all). And when you wake up in the morning, there is no time for a guy to scrape the oil from his hair or for a girl to "put her face on" before they see each other. On our trip, the polite veneer of dating decorum was peeled away, and in some cases what was revealed sent the couples to opposite ends of the bus, trying to figure out an escape plan—an exit strategy out of the relationship.

But it wasn't just physical realities that were unmasked; it was the emotional and spiritual ones as well. Most guys could overlook mussed hair, and most girls could forgive a scruffy beard or the need for a shower. Faces can be washed, hair can be combed, and makeup can be refreshed or restored. That wasn't the problem. It was the wear and tear on appearances and relationships that result from grueling weeks of exhausting travel.

Interestingly, Sarai's physical beauty survived and even seems to have thrived through the hard travel in a scorching, hot, desert sun. As she grew older Sarai was more beautiful than ever. Indeed, said Abram, "I know that you are a woman of beautiful countenance" (Genesis 12:11 NKJV)— and this was said when she was in her late sixties! Outwardly her beauty was undeniable, but inwardly her heart and character didn't match. Or, as the Motown group, the Temptations, used to sing, "Beauty is only skin deep, but ugly goes all the way to the bone." Her great beauty could not compensate for the emptiness in her heart.

A Woman with a Destiny

Sarai's physical appearance must have been something to behold. Even at ninety years of age she was so beautiful that Abram feared that her dazzling beauty would cause the local kings to fall in love with her and abduct her! Was this a case of Abram's vision being the first thing to go? Not at all. Pharaoh and Abimilech both desired Sarai because of her great beauty (Genesis 12:10–20; 20).

PERSONAL RESPONSIBILITY

Twice Abram resorted to deception because he felt threatened by his wife's beauty, and twice Sarai supported his plots—plots rooted in lies and lack of faith (Genesis 12:10–20; 20:1–18). Twice Sarai was a full partner in her husband's faithless deception. Abram devised the schemes, but Sarai was a willing co-conspirator in not trusting God.

Here's what happened in one of these schemes. Abram and Sarai had traveled to Egypt to escape a famine (Genesis 12:10–20). When they arrived, Sarai's beauty captivated the leaders of the nation and even came to the attention of Pharaoh himself, who sought to take her as his own. In return, Pharaoh showed kindness and generosity to Abram, swelling his wealth with cattle and servants, a major currency of the day. While the land of Canaan suffered under the weight of famine, Abram seemed to be doing very well in Egypt.

Unfortunately, Pharaoh was not doing as well. Because of the ruler's inappropriate pursuit of Sarai, God judged him and his household, and the Egyptian ruler rightly sensed that his calamities were the result of his relationship with Sarai. He summoned Abram, and after exposing the couple's lie, he deported them from Egypt.

Rather than trusting God to provide for them and protect them, they concocted a human scheme. Instead of leaning on integrity and truth, they depended upon ma-

175

nipulation. And in doing this, they began the deadly practice and pattern of resorting to human craftiness instead of
trusting in God's omnipotence.

We know that lying is a sin, but we live in such a way
that deception seems to be a "very present help in time
of trouble," says Howard Hendricks, Dallas Seminary
professor and renowned author and speaker. We not only
practice falsehood, we also train our children to follow
our example, whether it is the so-called "white lie" of having your child tell the caller on the phone that you are not
at home, or the full-blown deception of misrepresenting
your tax return information. Our children and grandchil-
dren observe and learn from our practices more than they
listen to our "preaching" of unpracticed values. As a result, we far too often see our children reproducing our
very worst characteristics.

This certainly was true in Abram and Sarai's family.
Years later their son Isaac would repeat their pattern of
deception with his own wife, Rebekah, and their grandson
Jacob would be known as a deceiver and a thief, stealing his own brother's blessing and birthright. The sins of
the parents were not visited upon their children, but were
embraced by them as a life pattern that would disappoint
any parent. (Few things in life are as painful as seeing our
children modeling us at our worst.)

PERSONAL PAIN

Another area where Sarai struggled to trust God was
in a deeply personal part of her life that affected her very
sense of worth: her barrenness. For women of Sarai's culture, infertility was an embarrassment and a shame; but far

176

above that, it was a deep heartache. The inability to have children was a pain that touched every emotion because it affected the very survival of the family. In a culture dependent upon crops for survival, children helped with the work when they were young and cared for their parents in old age. Sarai's infertility produced shame and embarrassment, pain and fear. But instead of allowing her struggles to drive her to God, she responded in all the wrong ways. Sarah could not accept her barrenness—certainly a difficult and heartbreaking challenge for any woman, then or now. More importantly, however, she was unwilling to trust God with her despair and unwilling to believe in His grace. Once again, she resorted to human schemes and manipulation.

Sarai suggested that her husband sleep with her handmaiden, Hagar, in hopes that the maid would become pregnant. "Perhaps I shall obtain children through her," Sarai said to Abram (Genesis 16:2). She wanted to give her husband a child, no matter what it took to get that done. This kind of arrangement was not uncommon in the ancient world, but that is not the issue. The issue is that Sarai and Abram had been called to a relationship of faith in God, but instead of resting in Him, in His purposes and His timing, they once again resorted to manipulation and scheming.

In a scene that seems more soap opera than Scripture, Sarai encouraged her husband to commit adultery! The thing that, arguably, a married woman fears more than anything else—unfaithfulness from her husband—Sarai actually planned and executed. This alone may be the best measure of how deeply she felt the pain of her barrenness.

Abram's response? Whether out of concern for his wife's heartache or out of a basic weakness of character, he slept with Hagar. As a result, Sarai got her wish, and, through Hagar, gave Abram a son—Ishmael. But those were only the immediate results. For out of Sarai's determination to give her husband a son, her lack of faith, and his willing participation in her scheme came destructive long-range consequences that continue to affect our world today, thousands of years later, in the Middle East. There, in the land Abram called Canaan, the Jews of Israel (the sons of Isaac) and the Arabs and Palestinians (the sons of Ishmael) still live in enmity. Still, they distrust each other's words and motives. Still, they take each other's lives. Every suicide bombing, every Israeli incursion into the West Bank region, every angry mob scene, every threatening word of hate and act of death traces its genesis back to Sarai's scheme. The selfishness of Sarai lives on in the anger and conflict of the descendants of Isaac and Ishmael.

PERSONAL BITTERNESS

Sarai is a classic illustration of the old adage, "Be careful what you ask for; you might get it." She wanted Hagar to bear a child for her husband, and she got what she wanted. Her plan worked. But she wasn't happy or content. Instead, she became bitter toward Hagar, Ishmael, Abram, and even God Himself!

Several years after Ishmael's birth and after God had changed Abram's name to Abraham and Sarai's to Sarah (Genesis 17:5, 15)—a change that denoted the covenant relationship God had formed with them and their offspring to come—God, in the form of a traveling pilgrim, stopped for a visit at the tent of Abraham. This is what theologians call a "theophany," an appearance of the invisible God in some visible form. Here, God appeared as a man accompanied by two angels.

As God visited with Abraham under the shade of his tent flap, He told him some amazing news: "'I will certainly return to you according to the time of life, and behold, Sarah your wife shall have a son.' And Sarah was listening in the tent door which was behind him. Now Abraham and Sarah were old, well-advanced in age; and Sarah had passed the age of childbearing" (Genesis 18:10–11 NKJV).

"Well-advanced in age" is the understatement of all understatements. Genesis 17:17 makes it clear that Abraham was one hundred years old, and Sarah was ninety!

"Passed the age of childbearing"? I can easily understand their disbelief. My wife and I thought we had finished having babies after our fourth child, Andy, was born. But six years later I was stunned when Marlene informed me that she was pregnant! Although we were nowhere near the ages of Abraham and Sarah, I have often referred to our fifth child, Mark, as "the child of my old age."

Yes, I can easily identify with Sarah's reaction to this news: "Sarah laughed to herself, saying, 'After I have become old, shall I have pleasure, my lord being old also?'" (Genesis 18:12). But even as I understand her response, I also remember that important spiritual safety tip: never, ever laugh at God!

Sarah laughed at the promises of God and at the God of the promise. But that wasn't all. When challenged by God for laughing, she lied about it to God Himself. Talk about going from the frying pan to the fire! She laughed and then she lied. Rather than admit that she doubted God's ability to overturn the effects of the aging process and give them a child, she denied laughing at the thought of bearing a child.

It was not just the human improbability of bearing a child at her advanced age that prompted Sarah's reaction. I am convinced that it was also her heart turned bitter by decades of disappointment. She and Abraham had traveled far together, both in miles and in years. They had lived together for nearly a century, all the time hoping for a child— a promised child—to share their life and to carry on their family heritage. Her own foolish schemes had brought her only unhappiness. Always her hopes were crushed under the weight of years. Sarah had been disappointed so many times—why should she trust God now? It was just plain laughable.

This is how a heart responds when it is bitter against God. It is not the laughter of joy and celebration. It is the laughter of cynicism and skepticism. It is the sardonic laughter of a heart that has given up and no longer believes.

PERSONAL RELIEF

Sarah laughed at God out of fear and pain and, ultimately, bitterness. But in His mercy and His covenant-keeping faithfulness, God did exactly as He had promised.

Sarah conceived and bore Abraham a son in his old age, at the set time of which God had spoken to him. And Abraham called the name of his son who was born to him— whom Sarah bore to him—Isaac. Then Abraham circumcised his son Isaac when he was eight days old, as God had commanded him. Now Abraham was one hundred years old when his son Isaac was born to him. And Sarah said, "God has made me laugh, so that all who hear will laugh with me." She also said, "Who would have said to Abraham that Sarah would nurse children? For I have borne him a son in his old age" (Genesis 21:2–7 NKJV).

Now Sarah laughed again, but this time she laughed in joy and celebration over the birth of her son, Isaac. This child was more than an answered prayer and a fulfilled promise. He was an expression of God's forgiving love and mercy. The miraculous nature of this birth declared to the heavens, "Quiet. God is at work!"

What a vivid reminder for all of us to trust God, not only in the moment, but for the journey as well. Our spiritual pilgrimage in this fallen world consists of an endurance run, not a sprint. It requires of us that we continue to look forward and to try to understand where God is directing our lives for the future. With patience we wait for Him to fulfill what He has declared in His time, just as the apostle Paul challenged us: "Let us not lose heart in doing good, for in due time we will reap if we do not grow weary" (Galatians 6:9).

How much patience? Well, Sarah was over ninety years old when God's promise to her was fulfilled. That takes some patience!

PERSONAL REVENGE

Finally having her most fervent wish and desire come true should have been enough to satisfy Sarah—at least you would think so. But not all of Sarah's joy and laughter bubbled forth in the right spirit; some of it was about getting even. She had lived with her barrenness for years, and it had shaped her perspective on life as well as her choices.

A character forged by decades of disappointment is not undone in a single event, especially when the evidence of the choices of her bitterness (Ishmael) was before her all the time. Sarah couldn't take out her bitterness, anger, and disappointment on God. Also, she would not be content until all evidence of her previous failures was removed. Sarah would strike at her "foe" and the child who jeopardized Isaac's position in the family.

Sarah needed a human target, and she found an easy one in Hagar, her maid. In fact, Hagar was a logical target. She had given Abraham his firstborn son and was enjoying the cultural prestige that brought. Not surprisingly, as Ishmael grew, so did Sarah's bitterness. Finally, when she could stand no more, she decided to rid their home of Hagar and Ishmael, the child of Sarah's own scheming.

Sarah had to have been filled with guilt about her own disbelief and the results of her manipulation, but instead of confessing it, she blamed God and tried to destroy the evidence! You can almost hear the anger and bitterness in her voice as she says to Abraham, "Cast out this bondwoman and her son; for the son of this bondwoman shall not be heir with my son, namely with Isaac" (Genesis 21:10 NKJV).

Again submitting to his wife's wishes, Abraham drove Hagar and his own son Ishmael out into the wilderness. He gave them some "food and a skin of water," but in reality, he abandoned them there to die.

Sarah's bitterness had produced a life, and now her bitterness wanted to end that life. It is deep bitterness and fear indeed that demand satisfaction by the death of the innocent. Such was the case with Herod when he ordered the death of all male children in Bethlehem under the age of two in an attempt to relieve his own fears (Matthew 2). For Sarah, the numbers were different, but the intent the same. And but for the intervention of God Himself, Sarah's bitterness would have killed Hagar and Ishmael. Human life is a high price to pay for a heart battered by personal disappointment.

I grew up in West Virginia, where the feud of the Hatfields and McCoys was part history and part legend. Much of the legend we know, especially that retold on television and in movies, is folklore, but the story itself is based upon an historical event. There really were two families who were at odds with each other, and there really were tensions and anger, and there really was a tragedy of lost lives and broken relationships. But the horrible twist came toward the end of the feud, when family members on both sides were forced to acknowledge that they couldn't even remember why they were feuding! The bitterness between the two families had taken on a life of its own and had become a self-fulfilling prophecy. Today, the hills surrounding the southern West Virginia town of Williamson are dotted with grave markers that stand as silent reminders that human life is a high price to pay for bitterness—a tragic life lesson that Sarah never fully comprehended.

Sarah died at age 127, and Abraham mourned and wept over her body (Genesis 23:1–20). No matter how much scheming and bitterness she had carried out in her life, her husband obviously loved her dearly. In fact, his cooperation in her schemes and hers in his shows that they were one in heart and mind. Though they were nomads, he bought land in which to bury her, and in which his own body would later be buried. There in Hebron, to this day, are the tombs of the patriarchs, a place still revered by the Jews and a place still contested by the sons of Ishmael and the sons of Isaac.

Sarah, despite her doubt and bitterness, became the mother of a great nation. She had been given these privileges by God's grace, but not because of any personal worthiness on her part. By grace hers was a life of remarkable opportunity, yet her own nursed grief and scheming bitterness kept her enslaved to a heart that did not fully enter into the adventure and the joy of the promises she had been granted. By failing to fully embrace the promise offered by the God of grace, she wrote for herself a eulogy that never quite measured up to the unparalleled privileges she had been granted.

A Woman with a Legacy

When we conclude the story of Sarah's life in the book of Genesis, not much good is readily apparent. But when we turn to another record, we discover that God remembers her for what she became, not for what she had been!

Sarah is one of only two women (the other being Rahab) mentioned in the list of heroes of faith in Hebrews 11: "By faith even Sarah herself received ability to conceive, even beyond the proper time of life, since she considered Him faithful who had promised" (11:11). Though she struggled much with doubt and the desire to manipulate, eventually "by faith" she experienced the miraculous blessing of God, and she was allowed to conceive in her old age.

And in 1 Peter we learn about another legacy of Sarah's life. For all of her faults and failings, Sarah nonetheless offered a pattern of beauty that Peter remembered far beyond her recorded shortcomings. This is more than just trying to not "speak ill of the dead." Here the apostle acknowledged Sarah's rich contribution, which could not be negated by her episodes of manipulation or resentment, for she had become a model of how to carry true beauty in a debilitating and destructive world.

> Your beauty should not come from outward adornment. . . . Instead, it should be that of your inner self, the unfading beauty of a gentle and quiet spirit, which is of great worth in God's sight. For this is the way the holy women of the past who put their hope in God used to make themselves beautiful. They were submissive to their own husbands, like Sarah, who obeyed Abraham and called him her master. You are her daughters if you do what is right and do not give way to fear (1 Peter 3:3–6 NIV).

Sarah is remembered as both beautiful and obedient. But her true beauty came not from her physical appearance, but from her faith. Sarah was strong-willed and determined, but she also displayed a submissive heart to her husband, and, in Peter's view, ultimately to God. And this golden thread of submissiveness is what the Holy Spirit honors in 1 Peter 3. True beauty, true obedience, and, finally, true faith.

Much of what we remember about Sarah is that she laughed at the wrong time. Fortunately, as she grew into her desire for faith and obedience, her life and her legacy changed. True beauty emerged where only physical beauty had existed before.

What will your life and legacy be? And what mark of beauty will be seen in you?

PRINCIPLES FROM THE LIFE OF SARAH

- External beauty is a poor substitute for the inner beauty of the heart.

- Manipulation and deception cannot replace walking by faith.

- Anger and bitterness will ultimately destroy—usually those closest to us.

- Length of life is not synonymous with spiritual maturity.

- We cannot escape the consequences of the choices we make.

- God can turn our bitterness and cynical laughter into beauty of spirit if we trust Him in the face of life's disappointments and uncertainties.

11

Stephen

THE FIRST MARTYR

Few events in the twentieth century rocked the evangelical world as much as the martyrdom of five young missionaries in the jungles of South America in January of 1956. Jim Elliot, Nate Saint, Roger Youderian, Pete Fleming, and Ed McCully had gone to the Ecuadorian jungles to reach the Huaorani Indians (then known as the Aucas). Initial contact was made with the tribe, gifts were offered to show the peaceful intent of the young missionaries, and a base camp was established on "Palm Beach," a wide spot beside the Curaray River where their light floatplane could land. The men maintained contact with wives and colleagues by means of shortwave radio, and their spirits were high for this new outreach opportunity. Then came the day when the designated time for their contact passed without any word from the five men. With a cloud of dread looming over them, a rescue team ventured into the jungle. When they arrived at Palm Beach, they found the remains of the destroyed camp and the massacred bodies of the five young men.

The world viewed these deaths as a waste. Young men with so much potential, so much to offer, had been lost to the world, and for nothing more than the conversion of a heathen tribe that was on its way to self-destruction anyway. Even within the Christian community there were cries of despair. How could this mission of mercy have gone so tragically wrong? These men loved Christ, lived for Christ, and longed to serve Christ. What a terrible loss for these men to have died so young. What a tragedy!

Foxe's Book of Martyrs chronicles the reality that "the blood of the martyrs is the seed of the church." Yet even after two thousand years of church history during which countless faithful servants have died because of their faith in Christ, and even after we have seen the powerful working of God in the aftermath of such horror, martyrdom still raises questions and confusion, frustration and fear.

Chuck Colson and others have suggested that one pragmatic proof of the death and resurrection of Christ is simply this: if the message of Christ were just some giant hoax, some conspiracy of silence, who among these "conspirators" would have been willing to die for it? Yet almost from the beginning, believers have died for their faith in the atoning work of Christ. Through the centuries countless men and women have contributed to the blood of the martyrs as they were put to death for the crime of being faithful followers of Jesus Christ. The first person to suffer such a death was a man named Stephen. His story is brief and painful, but filled with the experiential wisdom that God desires to use in building our walk with, trust in, obedience to, and love for Him.

A Man of Spiritual Character

I enjoy watching the National Football League draft each April, especially watching how my own favorite team, the Cleveland Browns, selects players. I enjoy listening to the so-called experts tell why certain players will be terrific professionals and why others will be dismal failures. For a sports fan it is fascinating television.

In years past when a team was drafting new talent, the only consideration in the selection of a player was the level of his athletic ability. In recent years, however, that has changed dramatically as an increasingly important criterion in the selection process has become the character of the athlete. Players who have had legal or moral problems while in college find their draft potential dropping. Each draft choice represents millions of dollars, and character issues can dramatically jeopardize the team's investment. The question is: why has character become so important?

In the world of modern professional sports, coaches must manage players who make five to ten times their own salary. This makes an already tough job virtually impossible. How can coaches begin to control players who are, literally, worth more to the team than *they* are? Coaches used to cut players who weren't fitting into the program, but now players get coaches fired because the coach isn't maximizing the eighteen-year-old multimillionaire superstar's self-perceived potential, or, in some cases, simply isn't being nice enough to him. It is a strange world, to be sure, where money and talent have supplanted responsibility and maturity. Such internal conflicts can disrupt a team both on and off the field, and can sometimes be the difference between winning and losing. The stakes are unbelievably high, and thus character has become the silver bullet for successful professional sports franchises.

What the sports world has only recently discovered was understood by the early church two thousand years ago: lack of character can create conflict; infusion of character can resolve conflict. It is this equation that first brings Stephen into view in the book of Acts.

In the Jerusalem church a controversy arose between the widows of Jewish descent and the widows of Greek descent (Acts 6). The conflict had to do with the way resources were being distributed by the church's ministry to widows. The Grecian widows felt they were being short-changed.

When the apostles, who were leading the church in Jerusalem at that time, were notified of the conflict, their solution was simple: put character into the equation. "Select from among you seven men of good reputation, full of the Spirit and of wisdom, whom we may put in charge of this task" (Acts 6:3).

Notice that their solution was not to find men skilled in logistics or distribution. They did not seek out men with a background in business or skill in management. The apostles knew that if the people were to have confidence in those who were entrusted with the oversight of the widows' ministry, those overseers must be "men of good reputation, full of the Spirit and of wisdom." It was completely about character.

When this plan was announced, it "found approval with the whole congregation; and they chose Stephen, a man full of faith and of the Holy Spirit, and Philip, Prochorus, Nicanor, Timon, Parmenas and Nicolas, a proselyte from Antioch" (Acts 6:5). Not only did the congregation agree that the resolution of the problem required leaders with character, they also knew exactly where to look for such individuals—and the first one listed is Stephen. Obviously they viewed him as the embodiment of spiritual character, and Luke, the writer of Acts, describes him as "full of faith and of the Holy Spirit."

The word that is translated *full* here is a word that meant "to be under the control of" or "to be driven by," in the same way that the wind fills a ship's sails and drives the ship forward. What was it that filled Stephen's heart and life, motivating him and moving him in his choices and decisions? He was filled with:

- Faith: Confident trust in the living God was at the heart of who Stephen was. Habakkuk prophesied that "the righteous will live by his faith" (Habakkuk 2:4), and Stephen's life evidenced that kind of commitment to trust and dependence upon God.

- The Holy Spirit: This is what Paul would later describe when he wrote, "And do not get drunk with wine, for that is dissipation, but be filled with the Spirit" (Ephesians 5:18). To be filled with the Holy Spirit is to be under the control of the indwelling presence of God so that the believer does His will and displays His fruit (Galatians 5:22–23).

These qualities marked Stephen as a vessel of honor for the Lord's work. He was a man controlled by faith and the Holy Spirit, which made him a man of spiritual character and a person who could be trusted with this particular ministry.

191

In Acts 6:7 Luke tells us the practical results of importing men of character like Stephen and his colleagues into the midst of ministry situations: "And the word of God spread, and the number of the disciples multiplied greatly in Jerusalem, and a great many of the priests were obedient to the faith" (NKJV).

What a profound impact these men of character had! The Word of God kept spreading, the number of disciples (the church) increased, and, surprisingly, the impact even reached out to the "religious opposition" as many of the Jewish priests came to faith in Christ! Stephen's influence did not end there, however. In Acts 6:8 we are given further details about his growing ministry with the early church: "And Stephen, full of faith and power, did great wonders and signs among the people" (NKJV).

Stephen displayed apostolic gifts, showing the effect of God's unique call in his life. Full of faith and power, he performed wonders and miracles, and spoke with such wisdom that people could not resist the power of the truth.

Here we see Stephen at his brightest—controlled by the Holy Spirit, an instrument of spiritual power, and an evangelist who was both winsome and wise. He had become a messenger of the cross, and that message, the gospel itself, would inevitably take center stage.

A Man of Spiritual Wisdom

"Don't shoot the messenger" is a well-known expression. If the news is bad, don't blame the person delivering the news. In a media-filled world of commentators, analysts, and talking heads, we are accustomed to having our bad news delivered by attractive, articulate, stylish reporters who want to be disassociated from the news they report. Journalistic objectivity is their rationale. But that rationale is one-directional in nature, for the fact is that when bad news comes, we often do remember who delivered it to us. From Walter Cronkite reporting the assassination of John F. Kennedy to Aaron Brown, in his first day on the job with CNN, analyzing the 9/11 attacks on the World Trade Center in New York, we remember. We remember who reported the story, but we don't hold them responsible for the bad news itself.

Such was not the case with Stephen. As his ministry grew he continued to proclaim the bad news of sin and the good news of Christ, and some in the listening crowd took exception to the news he was delivering. They could not out-reason or out-think him (Acts 6:10), so they began misrepresenting both the man and his message.

> Then they secretly induced men to say, "We have heard him speak blasphemous words against Moses and God." And they stirred up the people, the elders, and the scribes; and they came upon him, seized him, and brought him to the council. They also set up false witnesses who said, "This man does not cease to speak blasphemous words against this holy place and the law; for we have heard him say that this Jesus of Nazareth will destroy this place and change the customs which Moses delivered to us" (Acts 6:11–14 NKJV).

Essentially, they did not like the news so they decided to "shoot the messenger"! They could not cope with the wisdom of God's Word, so they tried to discredit it. Sound familiar? This is the typical response of men and women of this age to the wisdom of God. When a culture based on relativism is forced to face the absolute truth and authority of the Scriptures, when a culture based on situational ethics is challenged to consider the unbending standards of a God of righteousness, when a culture committed to religious pluralism hears the Savior say, "I am the only way," they ridicule, attack, even reject—but they cannot deal with it!

Paul describes this response in 1 Corinthians 1:

> For since, in the wisdom of God, the world through wisdom did not know God, it pleased God through the foolishness of the message preached to save those who believe. For Jews request a sign, and Greeks seek after wisdom; but we preach Christ crucified, to the Jews a stumbling block and to the Greeks foolishness, but to those who are called, both Jews and Greeks, Christ the power of God and the wisdom of God. Because the foolishness of God is wiser than men, and the weakness of God is stronger than men (vv. 21–25 NKJV).

But these enemies of truth were not content to spread rumors about Stephen and ruin his ministry. They accused him of blasphemy, arranged for false witnesses to testify against him, and dragged him before the Jewish Sanhedrin to be put on trial. The NIV notation on this passage points out the possibility that Caiaphas, the same high priest who engineered the kangaroo courts that tried Jesus, also was running the show in *this* travesty of justice.

When they began to question him, Stephen was remarkable. "All who were sitting in the Council saw his face like the face of an angel" (Acts 6:15). They were seeing the peace of God in the heart of God's servant doing God's will. They were seeing the face of an angel! Stephen had no advocate, no representative, no support group around him, yet he knew that he was not alone. He knew that God had not and would not abandon him!

As the religious leaders of Israel interrogated him, it was not Stephen but his message that was on trial. And in contrast to the frenzy and mob mentality that surrounded him, Stephen was calm and composed as he responded—and his response was brilliant! It was a careful recitation of key elements of the history of the people of Israel, followed by a pointed application that flew in the face of his accusers, the court, and the crowd. His message boiled down to two primary themes:

The History of Israel

Stephen doesn't pull any punches, but goes straight to the heart of the matter. He reminds his accusers of the call of God upon Abram, who, in faith, left his home to go to a Land of Promise. He reminds them of Joseph and the deliverance of Israel first into and then out of Egypt. He speaks of divine rescue through the leadership of Moses, and the establishment of the nation at Sinai.

At Sinai, however, the story shifts from God's faithfulness to Israel's unfaithfulness. Israel had been granted the privilege of a special relationship with God. Yet from the golden calf crafted at the foot of the mountain of the law to the prostitution of the temple in the days of the Christ, Israel had repeatedly turned away from the God of Abraham, Isaac, and Jacob to worship gods of their own making, whether a calf of gold or the temple itself.

The Gospel of Christ

Finally, Stephen turns his focus to the religious leaders themselves and their own place in this litany of rejection.

They have rejected their Messiah and stand guilty before God, he says. He makes no attempt to soften the blow of reality as he declares:

> "You stiff-necked and uncircumcised in heart and ears! You always resist the Holy Spirit; as your fathers did, so do you. Which of the prophets did your fathers not persecute? And they killed those who foretold the coming of the Just One, of whom you now have become the betrayers and murderers, who have received the law by the direction of angels and have not kept it" (Acts 7:51–53 NKJV).

And what was their response to this argument of spiritual wisdom? Hatred and bitterness! "The Jewish leaders were infuriated by Stephen's accusation, and they shook their fists in rage" (Acts 7:54 NLT). Here we see the unbelieving world's reaction to God's work. Conviction either hardens hearts or softens and breaks them—and these men refused to be broken or softened!

A Man of Spiritual Devotion

In contrast to their fury, Stephen's countenance is one of peace. He gazes into heaven and sees the glory of God and the Savior Himself! Enraptured by the sight, with a heart full of love for Christ, Stephen declares: "Look! I see the heavens opened and the Son of Man standing at the right hand of God!" (Acts 7:56 NKJV).

At Stephen's declaration of the glorified, risen Christ, the crowd loses it altogether! The young servant of Christ is controlled by faith and by the Spirit, but the mob is out of control. The same mob mentality that crucified Jesus is

196

at work here (Acts 7:57–58). In a rage, they cast him out-side the city walls and stoned him to death.

Yet even as he is dying at their hands, Stephen prays for them, following the example of the Christ Himself when He was dying on the cross. "While they were stoning him, Stephen prayed, 'Lord Jesus, receive my spirit.' Then he fell on his knees and cried out, 'Lord, do not hold this sin against them'" (Acts 7:59–60 NIV).

Stephen's final prayer reveals his:

- Great Peace: in his heart and revealed by his response to his own death.
- Giving Love: to those who killed him, asking God's forgiveness for their act of murder.
- Going Home: to the presence of the Christ, standing at the right hand of the Father to welcome him into heaven!

Why could Stephen respond this way to such obvious in-justice? Because of his character and spiritual life, because of the quality that caused him to be called into ministry in the first place: he was "full of faith and the Holy Spirit."

When faced with the most severe trials of life, "the fruit of the Spirit" is dynamic (Galatians 5). Love, joy, peace—Stephen manifests them all! Love for his killers, joy at see-ing Jesus, peace in the face of a horrible death. Did it make any difference? Well, consider: Saul, a young Jewish rabbi who "was in hearty agreement with putting [Stephen] to death" witnessed it all. And one has to wonder to what degree God used this event to prepare Saul for his soon-to-come Damascus road encounter with Christ!

A Man of Spiritual Witness

In the Christian community, and even in the world, the word *martyr* has come to mean "someone who dies for a cause." But this is a great misunderstanding, because the full meaning of the word goes much deeper than that. *Martyr* comes from the Greek word *martureo,* which has nothing to do with dying and everything to do with living. *Martureo* means "to bear witness." Because Stephen "bore witness" to the glory of Christ, he lost his life.

Stephen's martyrdom was not about dying for a cause; it was about being faithful to the gospel, even to the point of death. It was the same faithfulness and devotion that would cause Paul (formerly Saul) to declare, "For to me, to live is Christ, and to die is gain" (Philippians 1:21).

Of all the world's religions, Christianity alone teaches us not only how to live, but how to die. A tragedy? A waste? Perhaps to the eyes and values of the watching world. But look at the same tragedies through God's eyes and the window of eternity.

When Jim Elliot and his comrades were killed in Ecuador on January 8, 1956, the call went forth to Christian young people to pick up their fallen banner of spiritual commitment. Thousands from around the world stepped forward to join the cause of world missions, and countless people throughout the world, many in places formerly unreached by the gospel, have been impacted for eternity by their devotion—a devotion born of the loss of five young men taken before they could complete their mission. Beyond that, their mission to the Aucas was accomplished as Elisabeth Elliott and Rachel Saint stood in the gap for their fallen loved ones in the jungles of South America, leading the very killers of their family members to knowledge of the Savior.

When Stephen was killed, God was already preparing the heart of young Saul of Tarsus. Shortly after this event, when he was on his way to persecute more Christians, Saul would come into contact with the Savior Himself—and his life, his heart, and his mission would change forever. Saul of Tarsus, who started as a killer of Christians, became the apostle Paul, the greatest church planter of the first century, one of the great theologians and apologists of the church age, the writer of more than half of the books of the New Testament, and perhaps the most influential believer in the history of the church.

Never lose sight of what God can do through the times of gray and despair, for even those are opportunities for witness, for true *martureo*. He can cause the wrath of men to praise Him, and can take apparent tragedies and turn them into patches of God-light that shine brightly in this dark world.

◆

I had a college friend, Mac Rivera, who was instrumental in drawing me to personal faith and invested in my early spiritual growth as a friend and a mentor. Mac was a great athlete and a gifted speaker. His goal was to return to his hometown of Washington, DC, and build a dynamic church ministry in the midst of the African-American community there. That was his plan and his mission. I was in Louisiana with one of the college's ministry teams when we received word that Mac and his fiancé, Sharon, had been killed in an accident. Beyond devastated, I was disillusioned. How could a loving God allow such a pointless tragedy?

As I wrestled in my own heart with the validity of faith, another friend challenged me to try to see the eternal in this shocking loss. I honestly tried, but just couldn't see how Mac's death could serve the kingdom better than his life would have. Then we received another report from campus, this one relaying the details of Mac's funeral. At the conclusion of the funeral message a challenge had been given—and over 220 college students stepped forward to pick up the mantle from the fallen servant and committed to stand where Mac no longer physically could. I was awed at the power of God to take the pain of personal tragedy and accomplish glory from it. Almost thirty years later, I still am.

It isn't easy, this life of commitment to the Savior, just as it isn't easy to see potential giants for God taken at a time we feel is "too soon." No, it isn't easy. It isn't supposed to be. Although Mac's death was accidental, unlike the martyr deaths of Stephen and the five missionaries, it was no less painful and no less traumatic—and no less in need of someone to step into his place of future ministry. But for Stephen and Jim Elliot and countless others, dying "before your time" has sometimes been the price tag of witness. And for all eternity they will affirm that the results God brought through their early departures to heaven were worth it.

Every day we encounter people controlled by self-pity, or apathy, or greed, or lust, or bitterness, or self, or _____ (you fill in the blank). What fills you? What controls you?

When we hold a worldview based on faith not sight, controlled by the Holy Spirit and not self, the world calls us fools. But remember the words Jim Elliott penned in his journal: "He is no fool who gives what he cannot keep to gain what he cannot lose."

PRINCIPLES FROM THE LIFE OF STEPHEN

♦ The best instrument for the resolution of Christian conflict is the infusion of Christian character.

♦ What fills or controls us is what will define how we respond to the challenges and hardships of life.

♦ The faithfulness of Stephen in a secondary ministry brought him more significant opportunities to serve Christ in primary ministries.

♦ We should not always expect an unbelieving world to happily embrace a message of truth about sin and salvation.

♦ We must always respond with the compassion of Christ to those who respond to the gospel with anger, and even hatred.

12

Thomas

THE DOUBTER

When I think of Joe Montana, the great quarterback of the San Francisco 49ers in the 1980s and '90s, I don't think of a great passer—that would have been Dan Marino of the Miami Dolphins. When I think of Joe Montana I think of one thing—leadership. When I think of Pittsburgh Pirates baseball great Roberto Clemente, I think of completeness. Clemente, who graced baseball fields in the late 1950s through the early '70s, was a true "five tool" player—he hit for average, hit for power, fielded flawlessly, threw magnificently, and ran with reckless abandon. He was a complete player. When I think of Mary Lou Retton, Olympic champion gymnast from my home state of West Virginia, I think of energy—endless energy. That is the best way to describe the sweetheart of the Los Angeles Olympics who won the heart of a nation.

If you were asked to describe your spouse, a friend, a political figure, a great athlete, a spiritual leader, how would you do it? Probably you would use a variety of words, either negative or positive, to create a verbal snapshot of the person. You might identify character qualities or talents or physical attributes. You might describe accomplishments or failures or events. From your parents to your boss, from your best friend to your favorite singer, any personal description requires several words or phrases to get the point across clearly.

But not Thomas. (You know who I mean already, don't you?) Never has an individual been so completely identified by one word, and one word only! Whether as a human proverb or a religious punch line, we all know who is meant when we hear "Doubting Thomas."

But Thomas is certainly not alone in his struggle with skepticism. And in that sense, he'd feel right at home in our twenty-first century. Doubt, skepticism, and cynicism have been with us through the ages. But today, we in the United States seem to have become a nation of skeptics. Just examine our newspapers and magazines, listen to our television and radio programs, or read our advertisements and bumper stickers. Bill Maher, host of the controversial television show *Politically Incorrect,* says, "We need very much to be more cynical." A sign bearing the slogan of an accounting firm declares, "In God we trust—all others we audit." We don't even trust a "Wet Paint" warning. We have to investigate to make sure!

Today, people doubt their beliefs and believe their doubts. And this mentality has even seeped into the church, which seems a blatant contradiction to our calling as "believers" or as "people of faith." We should be able to benefit greatly, then, by examining the life of one man who learned the hard way to believe his beliefs and doubts his doubts. Because although there may be a measure of justification for Doubting Thomas's reputation, he did not end where he began.

The Initial Introduction

In one of the all-time best adventure movies, *Raiders of the Lost Ark,* from the very opening moments we are offered intense, spine-tingling drama and mystery as we enter the dense green jungles of South America. We see the expedition guides, we hear the jungle birds and animals, but the main character stands in the shadows. Then the music swells and a figure steps out of the mist and shadows . . . and, for the first time, we see Indiana Jones. His introduction is dramatic, to say the least.

No such drama occurs in our introduction to Thomas. In fact, in his first appearance he is merely mentioned in a list of other names! How boring and undramatic is that? Ah, but wait a minute. Being a part of this particular list was not an insignificant thing, and it was anything but dull, because this is the list of those Jesus chose to be His disciples. And there is Thomas, right in the middle.

And when He [Jesus] had called His twelve disciples to Him, He gave them power over unclean spirits, to cast them out, and to heal all kinds of sickness and all kinds of disease. Now the names of the twelve apostles are these: first, Simon, who is called Peter, and Andrew his brother; James the son of Zebedee, and John his brother; Philip and Bartholomew; *Thomas* and Matthew the tax collector; James the son of Alphaeus, and Lebbaeus, whose surname was Thaddaeus; Simon the Canaanite, and Judas Iscariot, who also betrayed Him (Matthew 10:1–4 NKJV, emphasis added).

Thomas was among the select few called by the Savior to be His initial ambassadors on the earth. He was one of those select few who were given the power to cast out demonic spirits and heal all kinds of sicknesses and diseases. He was one of the twelve men called to a unique personal relationship with the incarnate Son of God. And Thomas responded to that call with obedience and commitment. He followed the Christ and, in doing so, embraced all that it meant to do so.

Imagine for a moment that you are Thomas and you have just been singled out to follow Jesus. Excitement, wonder, and anticipation could not begin to describe your emotions of that moment. It was not uncommon in ancient Israel—and was a great honor indeed—for an itinerant teacher, or rabbi, to gather around him a small group of followers called *mathetes* (learners) who traveled with him and were the direct recipients of his teaching. But to be invited to live with, eat with, and talk with the great Rabbi from Nazareth—what an overwhelming opportunity and privilege! Following this Teacher was not hero worship or a desire to be seen with the "right" people. It was a desire to learn truth from the One who had come into this world "full of grace and truth" (John 1:14). What better place to learn?

Years ago, when I was a young pastor, I found myself responsible for all aspects of ministry in our new, small church. This meant that I spent a great amount of my time doing things I had not been equipped or trained for when I was in Bible college. One of these areas was the music and worship ministry of the church. Now, I had been involved in music ministry while in college, but was in no way prepared to direct music and worship and all that is a part of such an important aspect of the life of the church. I wasn't even certain, philosophically, what direction the music ministry of a church should take. To be frank, I didn't have a clue.

After a couple of years of floundering in the area of music and worship, I had an opportunity to attend a pastors' conference at a large West Coast church. As I sat in the worship services and experienced the wonderful expressions of praise that made up those events, I realized that the music pastor of that church understood far more than I ever had imagined was necessary for such an undertaking. I also realized that if I was going to learn about music and worship in the context of the local church, here was a man who could teach me. So I made an appointment with him, asked dozens of questions, and gained tons of insights. That was twenty years ago, and to this day, I credit that time for much of my ministry perspective on music and worship.

My learning experience that week at the feet of a master of music and worship, and the excitement and joy I felt as I went back to my church to lead that ministry, gives me a small sense of what Thomas must have felt. When Jesus called his name, Thomas knew that he would be spending his time at the feet of *the* Master. The next three years reinforced the awe and wonder of that special and precious experience as Thomas watched the Christ feed multitudes, heal hundreds, and teach the crowds. He saw the joy of a leper made whole and a prostitute forgiven. He saw the compassion of Christ as He delivered a demoniac and the passion of Christ as He confronted the religious establishment. No one could have had a better, more full-orbed training ground to prepare for ministry. And Thomas experienced it all.

The Preliminary Appearances

But what happened to Thomas during those years that he walked with the Savior? We have to look carefully for clues, because the record regarding Thomas is sparse to say the least. Outside the post-resurrection events for which he is notorious and the lists of the disciples that Jesus had chosen, Thomas is mentioned only two times in the gospels, and in both cases he is already playing the role of resident pessimist.

The first of these events took place when the tide of public opinion was beginning to turn against Jesus and there was real danger for Him in and around Jerusalem. In fact, Jesus had left Jerusalem and taken his men to the far side of the Jordan River because the controversy had become so great that some of the religious leaders wanted to stone Jesus to death (John 10:40). Then a messenger arrived, telling Jesus and the twelve disciples that their good friend Lazarus was very ill (John 11). When Jesus declined to go to His friend, the disciples undoubtedly gave a huge sigh of relief. After all, Lazarus lived in Bethany, just outside Jerusalem and very much inside the political danger zone. Two days later, however, Jesus shocked the disciples when He told them that they were returning to Bethany because "Lazarus is dead" (John 11:14).

Thomas's reaction is most revealing: "Thomas therefore, who is called Didymus [twin], said to his fellow disciples, 'Let us also go, that we may die with Him'" (John 11:16).

Okay, Thomas says. Our rabbi is going to get killed. So let's go with Him so that we can die with Him. Not exactly an upbeat perspective! We do have to credit Thomas for a devotion that drove him to follow Jesus even when he thought it was to the death. However, his fatalistic attitude did not make him the life of the party. Danger, yes. Certain death and destruction? Well, maybe that was a touch over the top. Thomas was definitely a "prophet of doom."

And the next time we hear from Thomas he is no more comforting or hopeful. In the upper room, the night before His crucifixion, Jesus offered the promise and assurance that He would return for His own with these words: "And if I go and prepare a place for you, I will come again, and receive you to Myself; that where I am, there you may be also. And you know the way where I am going" (John 14:3–4).

After three years of listening to Jesus speak of the Father and of the kingdom of heaven, it could be argued that Thomas and the disciples should have had a framework for understanding those words. But they did not, and it was Thomas who voiced their ignorance when he said, "Lord, we do not know where You are going, how do we know the way?" (John. 14:5).

So in addition to being a pessimist, Thomas was, at the very least, spiritually, a slow learner. When facing danger, he saw death. When offered promise, he saw disappointment.

By themselves, these rather brief glimpses might not prove much. But when Thomas steps onto center stage for his most significant appearance in the New Testament, these first impressions of his character are strongly reinforced.

The Main Event

Sometimes life is not about months or years. It is about moments. In the golf movie *Tin Cup*, Roy McAvoy, a struggling pro at a golf driving range in the wastelands of west Texas, has squandered a magical ability at the game through lack of self-control and abuse of alcohol. Motivated by love for a woman, he wants to prove his worth and find redemption for his wasted life, so Roy sets out on a bold attempt to qualify for the United States Open, the most prestigious golfing event in the world. Along the way, he has several flashpoints of opportunity that he refers to as "defining moments"—moments that make all the difference in who you are and what you become. "Either you define the moment," he comments to a friend, "or the moment will define you."

Thomas's defining moment became the moment by which all history would both judge and define him. The setting? Resurrection Day. The event? Jesus' first appearance to His disciples following His victory over the tomb.

In the Wrong Place at the Wrong Time

When Jesus appeared to His disciples in the upper room following His resurrection, "Thomas, one of the twelve, called Didymus, was not with them when Jesus came" (John 20:24). And what an opportunity he missed. Simply by not being in the right place at the right time:

- He missed the blessing of peace (John 20:19). "Jesus came and stood in their midst, and said to them, 'Peace be with you.'"

- He missed seeing the resurrected Lord (v. 20). "And when [Jesus] had said this, He showed them both His hands and His side. The disciples therefore rejoiced when they saw the Lord."
- He missed the commission of Christ (v. 21). "[Jesus] said to them again, 'Peace be with you; as the Father has sent Me, I also send you.'"
- He missed the promise of the Holy Spirit (vv. 22–23). "Then he breathed on them, and said to them, 'Receive the Holy Spirit. If you forgive the sins of any, their sins are forgiven them; if you retain the sins of any, they have been retained.'"

Woody Allen is credited with saying that "seventy percent of success is just showing up." Someone else has scaled that down to "half of life is showing up." I tend to agree. And when it comes to the Christian life, there is no substitute for just being available for whatever God might desire for our hearts and lives. David was available when no one else would take on the giant Philistine, Goliath. Noah was available for God's use when no one else was interested in a divine opinion on the status of humankind. Isaiah was available when God called, "Who will go for Us?" as he responded, "Here am I. Send me!" (Isaiah 6:8).

But Thomas didn't show up. We don't know what transpired during the hours after the crucifixion of Jesus, except that the disciples were hiding in fear. Then, on the first day of the week, Mary Magdalene burst into their hiding place to tell them that the Lord was risen! John doesn't tell us if Thomas had already left the rest of the group for some reason, or if he left—perhaps in disbelief—after hearing Mary's announcement. We only know that he was not with the followers of Christ later that evening when Jesus Himself arrived. It may not have seemed like a big deal not to be there—but what a big deal it was! Just think. What if . . .

- Peter had gone fishing on the Day of Pentecost?
- Elijah had steered clear of Mount Carmel?
- Daniel had gone along with the crowd instead of standing against the easy path of compromise?
- Ruth had not gone to glean in the fields of Boaz?

It is out of just such ordinary choices that extraordinary events can occur. And nothing is more ordinary than the simple choice to be available. Perhaps the easiest way to miss out on the blessings of God is to not be where He is working when He is working! And often the thing we miss is the thing we need most.

There is no substitute for disciplining ourselves to be faithful and consistent, to simply be there—wherever "there" is in the workings of God in your defining moment. To give a cup of cold water in Jesus' name. To offer a word of encouragement to someone who is struggling. To quietly and anonymously pray for people who hurt. To share the message of Christ with people who need eternity. To show up.

IN THE RIGHT PLACE WITH THE WRONG ATTITUDE

Thomas did show up eventually. He arrived after Christ had departed from the upper room, and must have been shocked by what he found. The band of men who had been mired in loss and depression for three days and three nights were now over the top with joy, celebrating the unthinkable, the unimaginable—and for Thomas, the unbelievable. "We have seen the Lord!" they said.

But as they began to gush with information about and descriptions of Christ's appearance, Thomas was decidedly cynical and skeptical: "Except I shall see in his hands the print of the nails, and put my finger into the print of the nails, and thrust my hand into his side, I will not believe" (John 20:25 KJV).

No backwoods naiveté for Thomas. No simplistic gullibility. He insists on proof—with an edge. You can hear the sarcasm as he demands to actually thrust his finger into the nail prints and his hand into the spear wound in the side of the Savior. He had seen the Christ crucified. Nothing but irrefutable proof—"let me see; let me touch"—would convince him.

Long before there was a "Show Me State," Thomas displayed the skepticism of a native son of Missouri. He was a twenty-first-century man in the first century. We are flooded with more and more information, but find ourselves believing less and less. We want proof—miles of surveys, tons of investigations, hours of testimony, millions of statistics. Yet even given that, we remain world-class doubters because we have been hardened by two powerful things:

- Humanity's failures. Over and over, in a multitude of ways great and small, men and women prove themselves unworthy of trust, and as a result find it foolish at best and dangerous at worst to trust anyone else! From Watergate to PTL, the scandals of politicians and television evangelists have caused us to automatically distrust anyone in authority, even those who are considered to be in positions of spiritual authority.

- Sin's byproducts. Deceit and dishonesty have become the operating capital of our age. We watch television ads and infomercials with a predisposition toward disbelief—a situation that is probably not improved when the television stations airing those infomercials blast you with disclaimers that the station (which is more than willing to take the advertiser's money for the time to air the ad) is not responsible for any of the claims that the advertisement is making!

It seems that the entire world is from Missouri! Yet, in this world of skepticism and doubt we are called to trust in something that we cannot see or touch or feel.

Thomas also was challenged to have faith in God, but he refused to believe what he could not prove (John 14). Let us not miss this important point however: although Thomas is the one labeled the doubter, his response was actually no different than the response of the rest of disciples when Mary and the other women told them that they had seen the Christ. Thomas was not alone in his initial disbelief, so what sets him apart as "the doubter"? I believe his failure was not so much his skepticism, but its hard edge and the bitter, disillusioned spirit it revealed.

The Ultimate Understanding

Like many of my generation, I grew up in church. I remember going to Sunday school and reading the comic-book-style lesson sheets and memorizing my catechism verses. I also remember the utter emptiness of heart that plagued me as I outgrew childhood and the church service and Sunday school classes that seemed to be childish in the midst of a very sophisticated world. Somewhere along the way the things I had tried to believe as a child had grown pointless. I had lost faith in faith. I no longer believed that there was anything to believe. All the things I had heard seemed like so many tales, and the pressing reality of a true and living God seemed irrelevant in the world in which I lived.

I went to college—and dropped out. I took a job—and later quit. Nothing seemed to fill my emptiness. My personal wilderness wanderings led me through a variety of experiences—all, I am sure, intended by God to get my attention—until I ended up, of all places, at a Christian college. Make no mistake about it; there was no spiritual motivation behind my enrollment. I wanted to play football and get away from home, and this was an acceptable route. What I had not anticipated was Macauley.

Macauley Rivera—Mac—and I lived in the same dorm, and over the first two months of the school year we became friends. As we did, I watched Mac's life—a life that validated all the things I had given up on. His faith was vibrant and his love for Christ real. His relationship with the Savior was personal, intimate, genuine, and growing. I had decided that no such thing was possible, but now I was confronted with living, breathing, and smiling proof that Christ was real and still transformed hearts and lives. Proof.

Proof was also what Thomas wanted. Eight days after the resurrection appearance that he had missed, Thomas was in the upper room with the rest of the disciples when Jesus came to them again in spectacular fashion. "Although the doors were locked, Jesus came and stood among them, saying, 'Peace be with you!'" (John 20:26 NEB).

The doors were locked, yet suddenly Jesus stood in their midst! This in itself would seem ample evidence that something way out of the ordinary was happening.

When Jesus appeared, He immediately confronted Thomas and his doubt-filled heart. But His confrontation was not laced with condemnation; it was filled with compassion. Notice how the Master dealt with Thomas's struggling heart:

> Then He said to Thomas, "Reach here your finger, and see My hands; and reach here your hand, and put it into My side; and be not unbelieving, but believing." Thomas answered and said to Him, "My Lord and my God!" Jesus said to him, "Because you have seen Me, have you believed? Blessed are they who did not see, and yet believed" (John 20:27–29).

Jesus could have rebuked Thomas. Instead, He reached out to him. Jesus could have treated His doubting disciple as an enemy. Instead, He offered Thomas evidence. His scars became the proof of hope and of promise—proof that He is not the God of the dead but of the living. The wounds of nails and spear validated the wonder that His call to faith was genuine, based in reality, and able even to survive death.

This was strong evidence indeed. It was as if Jesus were saying, "You want proof, Thomas? Here it is. Now will you believe?"

Imagine the tension in that room! What would Thomas do? How would he respond to this irrefutable evidence? And I cannot express how important his response was: for Thomas responded by *not* touching! Offered the very thing he had demanded, Thomas now saw no need for it. He responded by believing—and there is no other way to respond to the evidence of the Lord Jesus Christ.

In the Old Testament, the prophet Habakkuk took all of the law of Moses and the teachings of the prophets and reduced them to one pristine principle: "The just shall live by his faith" (Habakkuk 2:4 NKJV).

This truth gripped a young, fifteenth-century monk who was struggling with guilt and the burden of unforgiven sin. Trying to absolve himself through self-flagellation and religious devotion, he found himself growing increasingly desperate. Then Martin Luther discovered Habakkuk's spiritual principle and understood for the first time that the apostle Paul had made that singular principle the foundation of relationship with Jesus Christ: "The righteous will live by faith" (Romans 1:17 NIV). Confronted by the evidence of Scripture, Luther embraced faith in Christ—and launched the Reformation. One revelation of truth—"the righteous will live by faith"—and the world was changed.

This was the truth that Thomas had to embrace as well. "By faith" always has been, and always will be, God's expressed requirement for forgiveness. Jesus Christ has done the work; He only asks us to believe it. Thomas had doubted, and now the evidence of Christ's resurrection from death to life had removed all doubt. From that moment on he would live by faith as he declared Jesus Christ to be both Lord and God, and yielded himself to the Savior.

The Rest of the Story

For Thomas, the Doubter, this experience of faith resulted in a changed life. We see him next with some of the disciples on the shore of the Sea of Galilee, where Jesus had said He would meet them (John 21:2; Matthew 28:7). This time Thomas was where he should be when he should be there. After that, we see Thomas in the upper room (Acts 1:13). He is there because Jesus, just prior to His ascension, had instructed them to wait in Jerusalem for the promise of the Holy Spirit (Acts 1:4). Again he was where he was supposed to be when he was supposed to be there. Thomas was now operating in faith instead of doubt, and as a result was making better choices.

Those choices would lead Thomas into a life of ministry and service to the risen Christ. History tells us that Thomas was the first disciple-missionary to take the gospel to India, where tradition says that he was martyred for his faith. Things that Thomas had doubted before the resurrection became the very truths he was willing to die for after the resurrection.

What a change! This is exactly what Paul wrote about when he proclaimed, "Therefore, if anyone is in Christ, he is a new creation; the old has gone, the new has come!" (2 Corinthians 5:17 NIV).

New life born of living faith in a living Savior.

Something worth dying for.

Someone worth living for.

217

PRINCIPLES FROM THE LIFE OF THOMAS

◆ There is no substitute for a teachable spirit. (After living and learning in the presence of Christ Himself for three years, Thomas understood little.)

◆ There is no substitute for an available spirit. (Thomas was not where he needed to be at the critical moment.)

◆ There is no substitute for a humble spirit. (Thomas willingly submitted to the evidence of the resurrection of Jesus Christ.)

◆ There is no substitute for a willing spirit. (Thomas embraced faith rather than doubt, then went on to serve his Savior.)

EPILOGUE

As we have considered these supposedly "lesser lights" of the Bible, a passage of Scripture has been muttering to me in the back of my mind.

> For consider your calling, brethren, that there were not many wise according to the flesh, not many mighty, not many noble; but God has chosen the foolish things of the world to shame the wise, and God has chosen the weak things of the world to shame the things which are strong, and the base things of the world and the despised God has chosen, the things that are not, so that He might nullify the things that are, so that no man may boast before God (1 Corinthians 1:26–29).

I find great comfort in these words. It is helpful to know that God has a place in His plan for the folks who don't dwell on center stage. In fact, the God of all grace delights in using those of us the world might tend to ignore. He chooses vessels that are, in the eyes of the watching world, foolish, weak, and nothing special—and turns them into something useful and precious by His own care and love. He takes ordinary people and uses them to accomplish extraordinary things. He surprises the world by showing them what He can do in a yielded life.

I am grateful for that. I am grateful that God delights in making the ordinary useful and the plain remarkable. And seeing Him work in and through the lives of folks who seldom find their way to center stage should encourage each of us to be available, and to stay available, for His service.

May the Lord continue to build an army of ordinary people who, by grace, are ready for those moments of purpose when He chooses to cast the spotlight our way—so that He will be pleased by what we do.

NOTE TO THE READER

The publisher invites you to share your response to the message of this book by writing Discovery House Publishers, Box 3566, Grand Rapids, MI 49501, USA. For information about other Discovery House books, music, or videos, contact us at the same address or call 1-800-653-8333. Find us on the Internet at http://www.dhp.org; or send e-mail to books@dhp.org.

ABOUT THE AUTHOR

Bill Crowder, who spent over twenty years in pastoral ministry, is now Associate Bible teacher and Director of Ministry Content for RBC Ministries. In addition, Bill has an extensive Bible conference ministry in the States and internationally. He and his wife, Marlene, have five children. *The Spotlight of Faith* is his first book.